The Pen Turner's Workbook

by Barry Gross

Fox
Chapel Publishing

1970 Broad Street • East Petersburg, PA 17520
www.FoxChapelPublishing.com

When you read other acknowledgements and dedications you really do not understand just how much work goes into making a book. Now, when I read them I will have a greater understanding and appreciation of just what happens when creating a book!

I first need to thank Alan Giagnocavo for allowing me the possibility to produce this book and to my editor, Ayleen Stellhorn for guiding this book novice through the twists and turns (no pun intended) of creating this book. I want to thank Tim Mize for his inspiring and creative pictures, and finally to all the people at the Fox Family for helping me with all my "whimsical needs."

As far as the turning aspect of the book, my friend Ed Ryan has been unselfishly teaching turning to many students for over 15 years and deserves recognition and thanks for guiding me with my turning experience. Without Ed's "ABC's" of Tool Control, chapter four would be a more difficult subject to express to you the readers.

© 2003 Fox Chapel Publishing Company, Inc.

The Pen Turner's Workbook is an original work, first published in 2003 by Fox Chapel Publishing Company, Inc. This book may not be reproduced in whole or in part, by mimeograph, photo process, any electronic or mechanical device, or by any other means, without express written permission from the publisher.

Publisher	Alan Giagnocavo
Book Editor	Ayleen Stellhorn
Cover Design	Jon Deck
Desktop Specialist	Alan Davis

ISBN 1–56523–215-1
Library of Congress Preassigned Card Number:
2003107294
To order your copy of this book,
please send check or money order
for the cover price plus $3.50 shipping to:
Fox Chapel Publishing Company, Inc.
Book Orders
1970 Broad St.
East Petersburg, PA 17520
Or visit us on the web at *www.foxchapelpublishing.com*

Printed in China
10 9 8 7 6 5 4 3 2 1

Dedicated to my best friend in life, my wife, Lenora, who keeps encouraging and inspiring me to reach higher while never looking back! Without her unwavering support and encouragement this book would not be possible.

Table of Contents

Introduction
So, you want to turn a pen?

Certainly there have been other books written on how to turn a pen. However, all the other books assumed that you have a certain skill level already in place. My objective with this book is to provide a text that is directed toward both the novice, who has never made a pen, and to the experienced pen turner, who may be looking for a fresh approach to designing, making and finishing a custom pen.

In addition, I will assist and guide the individual who is undecided which lathe to purchase or who is unsure which turning tools are best suited for a particular pen style and material. Tool techniques will be demonstrated to avoid the dreaded "dig in." Safety equipment and dust collection will also be discussed.

Of course, wood selection will be discussed in conjunction with the use of alternate materials such as antler, plastics, acrylics, Corian, and the newer Polygem pen blanks. We will also look into alternate ways to prepare the same wooden pen blank to obtain three very distinct outcomes as well as the use of wood dyes and coloring agents for your wooden pen blanks.

And finally, now that you have made this wonderful one of-a-kind pen, we'll talk a little bit about how to market your pen to maximize your efforts.

With that said, we have a lot of work ahead of us, so let's get to work and make some dust.

—Barry Gross

Part One
Pen Turning Basics

Turning pens is an exciting hobby that will afford you hours of enjoyment. The thrill of creating something useful and beautiful with your own hands will keep you turning pens for quite a long time. Not to mention the variety of materials that are available to pen turners. Stunning pens can be turned in everything from wood to acrylics. This first section will teach you the particulars of mini-lathes, turning tools and basic pen turning techniques.

Chapter One
Setting Up Shop

Choosing a Lathe

Purchasing a lathe is a personal choice, and one that can not be made solely on the recommendations of others. When considering the possible purchase of a lathe, take time to reflect and ask yourself the following questions.

• **What type of turning will you want to accomplish?** Lathes come in a variety of sizes and styles, and it is important to identify the type of turning you would like to do before you make a purchase. Investing in the wrong type of lathe can limit the number and types of pieces you can create. And if you're a beginner, the wrong type of lathe can make your first turning experience less than wonderful.

For this book, I'll be using a mini-lathe. As the name suggests, mini-lathes are smaller than regular-sized lathes and are particularly well-suited to smaller projects such as pens, pencils, ornaments, smaller bowls, hollow vessels and bottle stoppers.

• **Will you concentrate your energies strictly on pens?** Turning is a great hobby, and even if you only turn pens, there will be more than enough pens to keep you very busy. Pens come in all shapes and sizes and can be made from a variety of materials including, but not limited to, all sorts of domestic and exotic hardwoods, plastics, antler, bone and solid surface substances like Corian®.

In this book, you will learn how to turn five different pen styles. You will also learn to turn a sampling of some of the most common materials used in turning pens. Using your imagination to combine styles and materials will keep you busy with a never-ending array of projects for your new hobby.

• **Are you interested in turning smaller bowls or vessels now or possibly in the future?** As mentioned, the mini-lathe is a great tool for a variety of additional, small projects, including miniature bowls, perfume bottles, money clips and more. If you are even remotely interested in expanding your hobby to include more than pens, you'll want to take that interest into consideration when you make your lathe purchase. (Please note: Those additional items are not addressed in this book.)

• **How much money are you willing to commit to your purchase?** Mini-lathes vary greatly in price depending on the manufacturer and the accessories included. General pricing can run anywhere from just

Pen Tip

• **Make sure your lathe is fastened securely to your working surface.**

• **Decide what features are important to you and make sure the lathe you choose has those features.**

• **Only choose a lathe after you have tried turning with it.**

around $100 to hundreds of dollars. Again, think long and hard about how you want to use your lathe. Buying a more expensive lathe now may be a better use of your money than buying an inexpensive lathe now and a second, more expensive lathe shortly thereafter. (A sampling of mini-lathe manufacturers is listed in the back of this book.)

• **How much room do you have to devote to your lathe?** Mini-lathes are just that: miniature lathes. They measure about three feet across and about a foot or so deep. They are perfectly suited to small workshops, such as those in a garage or corner of a basement. My mini-lathe fits comfortably in my one-car garage, and it shares space with a dust collector, a band saw, a scroll saw, a wide variety of shop tools and uncounted blocks and boards of wood that will soon turn into beautiful lathe or scroll saw projects.

Tips for Choosing a Mini-Lathe

1.) Visit woodworking outlets and inspect the lathes for the features that are important to you.
2.) Check the internet for reviews of the lathe you are interested in purchasing.
3.) Personally test as many lathes as you can. Do not just let the salesperson demonstrate the lathe to you. In most cases the salesperson will be very proficient on his or her piece of equipment.
4.) Turn the lathe on and listen to it. Ask to change speeds on a belt-driven lathe by changing the belt (now you will see how difficult it is to change the speed) or by using the dial on a lathe with a variable speed control.
5.) Place your hand on the headstock and note how much vibration the lathe is generating. Now, conduct the "point to point" test. Place a point in both the headstock and the tail stock and run them together. Turn the lathe on and check it for accuracy. If the points do not line up precisely point to point, even while running, walk away and do not look back—even if the salesperson is offering a "great" deal. Remember the old axiom: It is always best to afford the best you can, because quality usually is reflective of the price.
6.) Finally, check that the lathe you intend to purchase is manufactured by a reputable company and find out exactly what the warranty includes.

• **Are you interested in a floor-mounted lathe or a bench-top lathe?** Your choice of a floor-mounted lathe or a bench-top lathe is determined by your workspace. If you choose a bench-top lathe, make sure the bench is positioned correctly so that you aren't turning too low or too high. Make sure that your lathe is bolted to your benchtop to avoid vibration. A floor-mounted lathe should have a sturdy mount, preferably one designed for this particular purpose.

• **Do you want a belt-driven lathe or one with variable speed control?** Both of these lathes are of such quality that the only advantage or disadvantage to them is time. Switching belts can take time out of your schedule, and if you are someone who has only a limited amount of time to turn, you may opt for the variable speed control.

Ancillary Workshop Machinery

The following equipment is not necessary but it is nice to have in order to save you time in preparing your pen blanks.
Drill press and drill centering vise: Used to center and drill the holes in your pen blanks for the brass pen tubes
Pen mill: Used to square the end of the pen blank to the barrel of the pen tube
Hand drill: Used in conjunction with the pen mill to square off the pen blank
Bandsaw: Used to cut the pen blanks
Grinding system: Used to sharpen turning tools

A drill centering vise, as shown here, is a handy extra around the shop. It will precisely drill the pen blank and minimize wandering of the drill bit.

A skew is a difficult tool to master, but once you have learned how to use it, it will become a heavy hitter in your arsenal of turning tools.

Selecting Pen Turning Tools

There are many manufacturers of turning tools today. Search the internet for turning tools and you will be inundated with information on kinds of tools and the numerous companies who make them. You will find each company claims that its tools are the best and will give you the cleanest cut while holding an edge longer than any of its competitors. The reality of the situation for today's turning needs is that you have two choices. You can choose carbon steel tools or you can choose tools made of high-speed steel (HSS).

Carbon steel tools are just that: tools that are made from carbon steel. These tools are not as expensive as tools made from high speed steel. They will keep a sharp edge for a short amount of time depending on the material that you are cutting.

There are many various grades of high speed steel.

They are identified by M1, M2, M7 and M50, with M1 being the most expensive grade and also the most brittle. Today, most of the HSS tools are made from M2 grade HSS or better. When turning woods and plastics, all grades of HSS tools will far outlast the lesser expensive carbon steel tools. On the average, high speed steel tools will hold an edge up to six times longer than carbon steel tools.

Now that you have selected which steel you want, which manufacturer do you choose? There are many reputable manufacturers of turning tools. Here again, the internet can be a valuable resource in choosing the correct manufacturer for yourself.

The basic turning tools that I recommend to my students are sometimes packaged as a set or purchased separately. The HSS set of pen-making tools below consists of a ¾" roughing gouge, ½" spindle master (a unique tool that is a cross between a skew and a spindle gouge) and a ⅛" parting tool. This is a basic pen set for anyone interested in turning pens.

The next two tools purchased would be a ¼" spindle gouge and a ½" skew. The skew is called the "white knuckle" tool because it is a difficult tool to master when you are just beginning your turning experience. However, the skew is a very valuable tool and can be used for many purposes including extra clean finishing cuts. With a little practice this tool will become a very valuable part of your turning arsenal.

With just these five tools, you will be well-equipped to turn any pen.

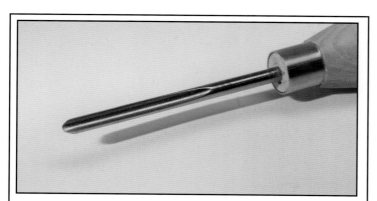

A spindle gouge is used primarily for turning beads and coves on pens. It is a good addition to a beginner's toolbox.

A basic pen turning tool set for beginners includes a parting tool, a spindle master and roughing gouge.

Safety in the Shop

We all know what is safe and what can be dangerous when working in the shop. However, the reality is we do not always practice what we know to be the right thing to do! When it comes to a lathe, it is important to do the right thing, or you can get into trouble very fast. By observing the following safety tips, we all can have a safer work environment to spur the creative genius inside every one of us.

Wear protective eye glasses and/or a full face shield. This is the most obvious safety tip, and, believe it or not, it is also the one that is most ignored. It only takes one small chip to scratch your cornea.

Do not wear loose clothing or have long hair dangling around your work in progress. Pull your hair back by putting it in a pony tail or under a hat. Remove any loose jewelry. Tuck in shirttails and roll up sleeves. Do not lean over the lathe while it is running, because it may catch your clothing.

Do not touch your work while it is in motion on the lathe. This sounds simple, but people still have a tendency to touch their work piece while it is still in motion. If you must touch it, do so lightly and on the top of the work. Never touch the piece in front of the tool rest where you finger can get caught in between the tool rest and the work piece.

A comfortable stance is important when you are working at your mini-lathe. Stand with your feet about shoulder's width apart. Your elbow should be even with or slightly above the level of the piece you are turning.

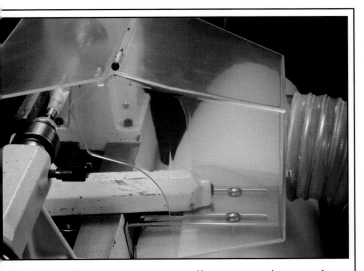

A dust collection system will remove dust and chips from the air as you turn. Coupled with a dust mask, this combination will provide solid protection for your respiratory system.

Dust collection of some form is a must! The dust collector located near the lathe will remove most of the airborne dust particles as you are turning and sanding. It utilizes a hood that is connected to the back of the lathe and offers strong suction to draw dust away from the operator. A stand alone dust mask used in conjunction with the above system will offer solid dust protection to the operator. Keep in mind that some woods can be toxic to individuals who are sensitive to particular woods, such as cocobolo and many spalted woods.

Be relaxed in front of your lathe. A good starting position should be with your feet about shoulder width apart. The center line of your pen should be slightly above or equal to your elbow when your arm is in a resting position by your side.

Proper lighting is a must. You have to see your work before you can effectively turn your work.

Chapter Two
Choosing Turning Materials

Trees, a pen maker's friend

According to the Greek legend, the Greek god Adonis was said to have been born of a tree. He gave to humanity the strength of the woody core, the upward reaching soul of the sky-seeking branches, and a rooting deep within Mother Earth that ties our hearts to the center of the world.

Trees are the longest living and largest living organisms on Earth. Currently the world's tallest tree is a Coast Redwood tree from California standing over 360 feet tall. The Bristlecone pines located in the United States are confirmed to be the world's oldest trees with ages up to 4,600 years old.

Numerous sources have stated that the actual number of tree species may well exceed 50,000. Since the beginning of time, trees have played a significant part in the survival of mankind. In 50 years one tree can recycle more than $37,000 worth of water, provide $31,000 worth of erosion control and $62,000 worth of air pollution control. Just two mature trees provide enough oxygen for a family of four and assist in reducing the "greenhouse effect" by absorbing carbon dioxide. Trees are excellent noise barriers, making neighborhoods quieter from highway noise. For patients in hospitals, a view of trees out their hospital window provides a soothing effect. Trees also provide us with food. And for the wood turner, trees are also an excellent material for wooden pens.

A quick dissection of a tree will provide you with some useful information about choosing and using wood in turning pens. First, the outer bark of a tree is a corky material that protects the main trunk of the tree. Directly beneath the outer bark is a layer of inner bark called phloem. The phloem is made of tubes that transport food and sugars throughout the tree. Inside the phloem is the cambium layer of the tree, which usually feels

Because of the way burls grow, they often have very interesting grains. Note the swirl pattern and the raised bumps, or "eyes," in this close up shot of a maple burl.

slimy in a freshly cut trunk. The cambium layer produces phloem (bark tissue) and xylem (wood tissue). The living xylem cells, called sapwood, carry water and minerals from the roots to the leaves. The sapwood lies in a broad ring around the darker heartwood and often is whitish or cream colored. As the sapwood cells die, they fill with organic material and become the heartwood of the tree which is the darker inner portion of the tree.

Now that you know enough about a tree's anatomy to be dangerous, which portion of the tree makes the best looking pen blank for the woodturner's needs? Sapwood or heartwood or combinations of both make impressive pens. Burls, which are growths on the trunks of trees, make stunning pens. In addition, grain direction can come into play. Straight grain, cross grain or end grain adds three more options. When it comes to wood choice, "so many choices, so little time" is the phrase that comes to mind. Let's take a closer look at some of those choices.

All trees are susceptible to burls. This is a photo of a burl from an oak tree.

Burls

The most desirous of all materials, in this author's opinion, is the burl. We all have seen them, but most of us have probably overlooked them not knowing what they were.

So, what is a burl and how do I find one? According to the Merriam-Webster dictionary, a burl is "a hard, woody, often flattened, hemispherical outgrowth on a tree." Basically, a burl is a benign tree tumor. Burls start to form when a twig bud cell fails to grow normally to form a limb. Instead the bud cells just continue to multiply and multiply, growing in a round growth with an irregular grain pattern. This is not good for the tree, but it is a great natural phenomenon for turners.

This photo shows a slab of cocobolo wood that includes both heartwood and sapwood. The inset photo shows two pens that were made from this piece of wood. The top pen was made without the sapwood, while the bottom one is part heartwood and part sapwood.

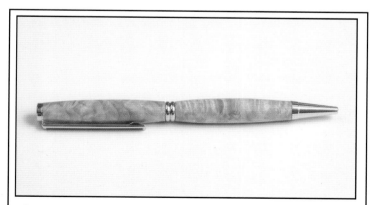

The unusual grain pattern of burls lends itself to stunning pens. In the author's opinion, there is no better wood for pen turning.

By cutting the blocks of wood at three different angles, you can get three very different looking pens. These three pens were all cut from the same piece of zebrawood.

Cutting on angles

Just because you use the same wood for a dozen pens does not mean that all the pens look identical. One way to get more variety out of your wood supply is to cut the blanks for your pens on different angles. Cutting on a different angle will cause the grain to run in a different direction, which will cause your pens to look very different.

Take a close look at the three pens in the above photo. These three pens were all made from the same piece of zebrawood. However, the pen blanks were prepared three different ways. The pen blank on the left was cut across the grain, the middle blank was cut on a 15 degree angle, and the blank on the right was cut parallel with the grain. While it's obvious that the three pens are all zebrawood, the look of each pen is unique.

Another example of a wood that looks very different when cut on an angle is cocobolo. Cutting the pen blank on a slight angle of approximately 15 degrees opens the grain up giving the pen a dramatic effect. If you end up selling your pens, the dramatic effect of this cocobolo pen will make it a very hot item.

Look at the bird's eye maple example in the center photo. The pen blank on the bottom is running parallel to the grain. The blank directly above it will be cut on an angle to open the grain up to offer a

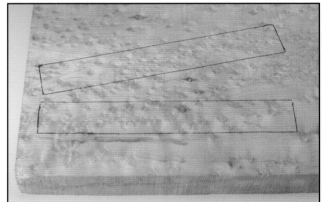

This piece of bird's eye maple will be cut two ways: once along the grain and once at a 15 degree angle to create two unique pens.

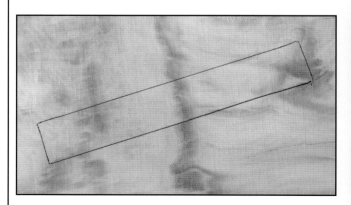

The red coloring running through the wood is actually the result of a disease.

Use the "look small" test to see if a piece of wood will look good as a pen blank. Simply hold a piece of acrylic the same size as a pen blank over the area you are considering and think small. This is a piece of cocobolo wood.

more enhanced grain in the finished pen.

The box elder slab shown to the left will be cut on an angle as marked. Note how the grain appears to be more open because the blank was prepared on an angle.

Knowing what looks good

As I said before, there are many, many choices of woods and grain patterns. One problem we have as pen makers is that often times we do not think small. A very beautiful piece of quilted maple with a lot of character may look spectacular as a large table. However, when reduced to the size of a pen blank, you probably will not get any of the quilting, and thus, your pen blank will appear very boring.

When considering any wood for a pen blank, you must be able to picture that particular material in a ¾" by ¾" pen blank. If you are not sure if a piece of wood will look good as a pen, put it to the "look

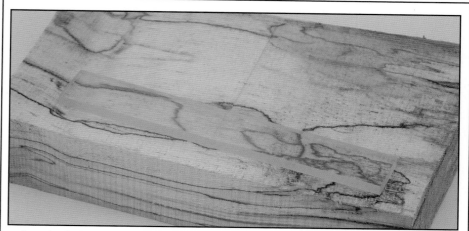

The dark lines in this piece of spalted maple will make a unique pen.

The grain in this piece of fishtail oak will create a interesting pen.

small" test. Take a piece of clear acrylic ¾" wide by 5¼" long and lay it over the piece of wood you are considering. If the piece of wood you chose has a lot of character, or if you see a lot of grain underneath the acrylic, then it probably will make a great looking pen. Remember: Think small!

Alternate Materials

Here again there are many types of alternate materials that can be turned into pens. You are limited only by the types of materials that can be turned on a lathe. I routinely turn pens from blanks of Corian, acrylics and antler. Additional materials include Dymondwood, Inlace, Polygems, and many others too numerous to mention. Remember if it looks good with your clear pen guide then it will probably make a good-looking pen.

Corian is a solid surface substance that is commonly used for kitchen and vanity countertops. It is easy to turn and creates an interesting pen that feels good in the writer's hand.

Natural materials such as buffalo horn and antler from deer and elk can also be turned into pens. The resulting pen has a translucence that is not duplicated in any other material I have found.

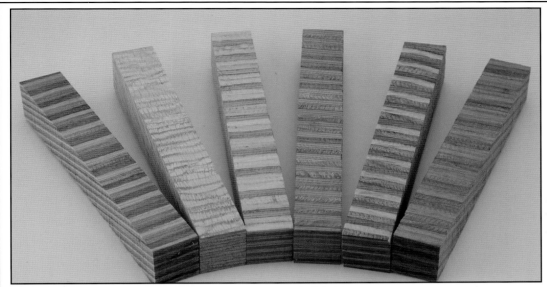

Dymondwood, although some find it difficult to turn, makes very interesting and appealing pens.

InLace is a unique acrylic compound that comes in a variety of colors. Pens turned from blocks of inlace are popular among pen buyers because of their interesting color combinations.

Yet another interesting material is Polygem. This acrylic compound mimics the colors of stones, minerals and gems that appear in nature.

Chapter Three
Pen Blank Preparation

Once you have chosen your material, be it wood, acrylics, antler or Corian, you must now choose which type of pen you want to turn. To date, there are well over 50 different styles of pens from which you can choose. No one particular style of pen will suit everyone, which is why there are so many different sizes and styles of pens. If you plan to sell your pens, you will want to make a wide variety to reach as many people as possible.

The additional parts that make up a pen, such as the bands, the clips and the ink barrels are sold in pen kits. These kits are available from many sources including woodturning supply stores.

The best way to find out where to purchase pen kits is to check the advertisements and classifieds in your favorite woodturning magazine or to do an internet search.

Throughout the pages of this book you'll find a number of different pens shown, including slimline pens, cigar pens, Euro or designer style pens, comfort pens, classic pens, roller ball pens and click pens. This is just a sampling of the pens you can turn on your mini-lathe.

Preparing the blank

The method of preparing a pen blank is the same, no matter what material you are using or what pen you chose.

Pen Tip

• Mark your pen blank for proper orientation before it is cut to length.

• Use a pen vise to drill your pen blank.

• To avoid a "blow out" when drilling acrylics, relieve the debris often.

Gather your materials

Open the pen kit and arrange the parts as per the instructions for the kit. (See Figure 1.) Most pen blanks will be at least ½" to ¾" square and 5¼" long. Each pen kit gives you the exact dimensions you will need for that particular pen blank. A quick way to measure this is to remove the pen tubes, place them on the material of your choice, then cut them to the proper length adding approximately ¹⁄₁₆" to each each end. (See Figure 2.)

Matching the pen blank

Once you cut your pen blank into two pieces, you will have to keep track of which end will be the top half of your pen and which end will be the bottom half of your pen. (See Figure 3.) Before you cut the blank in two, place orientation marks on the blank. If you are making more than one pen, mark each blank with its own designation. In Figure 3, note that the Bocote pen blank on top is cut on an angle, whereas the bottom blank is cut with the grain running parallel. Both blanks have distinctive marks for each pen blank. A rubber band can be used to keep multiple pen blanks together or you can make a holder such as the one shown on the next page. (See Figure 4.)

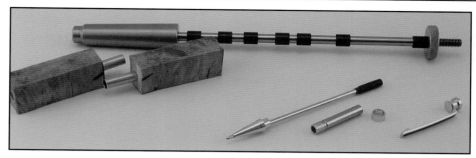

Figure 1: Pen kits include all of the hardware you'll need to make a pen.

Figure 2: Use the tubes to correctly measure and mark the pen blank.

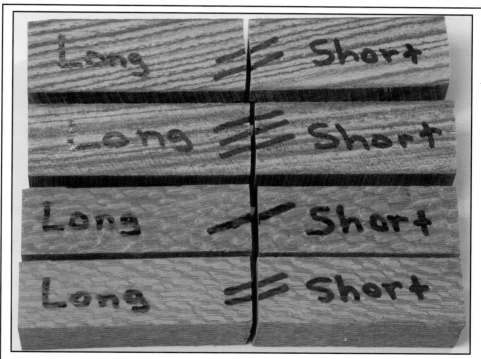

Figure 3: Avoid confusion by labeling the pen blanks clearly.

Drilling the pen blank

Holding a pen blank by hand and trying to drill straight through at a 90° angle is difficult if not impossible. The best way to drill a pen blank is to use a pen vise. (See Figure 5.) The blank is placed into a pen vise for two main reasons. The first is to precisely drill the blank, and the second is to minimize the wandering effect of the drill bit.

First draw a diagonal line from corner to corner to find the exact center of the pen blank (See Figure 6.); then, insert the blank into the pen vise. Drill at a continuous speed using a slight downward pressure. Relieve the debris from the blank often. This will

Figure 4: A simple stand such as this will keep pen blanks in order.

Figure 5: A pen vise will ensure an accurately drilled hole.

Figure 6: A simple X drawn from corner to corner will help you to find the center of the blank.

assure you the greatest chance for a clean and straight bore.

Problems can occur when too much pressure is applied and the debris is not removed often. This allows excessive heat to build up inside the pen blank. When excessive heat builds up too rapidly, it will cause a "blow out" as shown in Figures 7 and 8. This problem can occur in both wood and acrylics. Sometimes, a blow out is the result of either a dull drill bit or an incorrect bit. When this occurs, more pressure is usually applied to the pen blank causing more heat to be generated, thus causing a vicious cycle to occur.

A simple, common sense solution to the above situation is to use a good quality drill bit. The following two styles of drill bits, when used properly, offer excellent results. The first is a brad point drill bit and the second is a high speed steel twist drill bit. (See Figure 9.) All materials can be drilled with either of these two drill bits; however, the brad point drill bit is mostly often used for wood, and the HSS twist drill bit is used for all the other acrylic materials.

Gluing the pen tubes

After the pen blank is drilled, the next step is to glue the pen tubes into the blanks. These tubes are always made of brass, and their function is to hold the pieces of the pen together as well as to encase the pen cartridges inside the pen.

Before the tubes are glued into place, the tubes have to be "roughed" up. (See Figure 10.) Take the tubes and rub them against a piece of sandpaper to scratch them. This action gives the glue a better surface to which to adhere. Another method to rough up the tubes is to use a wire brush. A third method involves placing the pen tubes on a mandrel, then turning on the lathe while placing a piece of sandpaper against the tubes. Any method that scratches the brass tubes will suffice, so long as they are thoroughly scratched.

There are several types of glues that can be used to glue the tubes inside the pen blank. The two types of glues used most often are the Cyanoacrylate, or CA, glue (Super Glue belongs to this group) and the epoxy type of glue. CA glue is offered in three thicknesses: the first is a very thick gap-filling type of glue, the next is a medium thickness, and the last is thin. The medium and thin CA glues are the most popular glues for pen making. (A word of caution about CA glue: It does not discriminate between wood and fingers.)

For all wooden pens, the thin CA glue should be used first to coat the inside of the pen blank. (See Figure 11.) This is done for two reasons. If the wooden pen blank is porous, the thin CA glue gives the interior of the pen a better surface to which the medium CA glue can bond. It will also penetrate the wood blank, giving the finished pen some additional strength. To apply the thin CA glue, allow several drops to fall into the hole in the pen blank while turning the blank and allowing the CA glue to coat the inside of the tube.

Place the pen tube on the insertion tool and pour some medium CA glue onto a piece of wax paper. Coat the outside of tube with the medium CA glue; then, insert the pen tube into one end of the pen blank, going in and out to coat at least one half of the inside of the blank. Now reverse the tube and repeat the procedure on the other half of the pen blank. When you are finished, make sure that the pen tube is placed far enough inside the pen blank. (See Figure 12.) You may choose to spray some CA accelerator on your pen blank at this time to speed up the drying time of your pen blank.

The preferred method of gluing green or wet wooden pen blanks is to use epoxy glues rather than CA glue. Follow the mixing instructions for the specific epoxy glue and then use the guidelines as listed above to glue the pen tube into the pen blank. The reason for this switch in glues is that the moisture inside the green pen blank sometimes accelerates the drying process of the CA glue. The quick dry time will not allow you to place the tube inside the pen blank to the proper depth before the glue dries. You will be stuck with the pen tube half inside and half outside the pen blank. The use of epoxy glues on not-yet-dry pen blanks will usually offer you more time to place the tubes into the pen blank.

Squaring the pen blank

Now that the tube is glued into the pen blank, you must "square" the end of the pen blank in preparation for mounting the blank on a mandrel. Both ends of the pen blank must be square to the end of the brass tube inside the pen blank. This can be accomplished either by using a disc sander or with the use of a special tool called a "pen mandrel" or a "barrel trimmer."

Figure 7 (top) and Figure 8 (middle): Blow outs can occur from excessive heat buildup or dull drill bits.

Figure 9: A brad point drill bit (left) is ideal for drilling wood, and a high-speed steel twist bit (right) is perfect for all other materials; however, both bits will cut all materials.

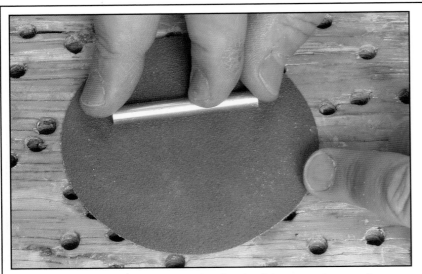

Figure 10: Rough up the tube by holding a piece of sandpaper still and rubbing the tube back and forth.

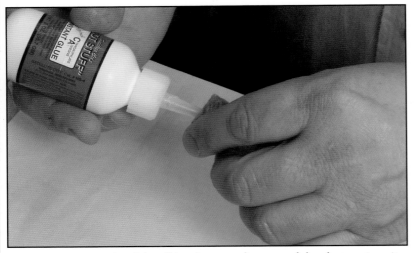

Figure 11: Apply thin CA glue to the pen blank to give it added strength.

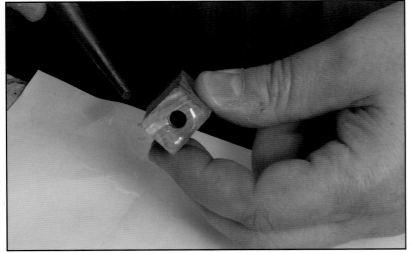

Figure 12: An insertion tool is used to place the tube in the blank.

The easiest way to trim the ends of the tube is with the use of the barrel trimmer. (See Figure 13.) Each particular pen kit will use a different barrel trimmer depending on the interior diameter of the pen tube. By using a barrel trimmer of the appropriate size, two tasks will be accomplished. First, the inside of the pen tube will be cleaned of any glue that is present inside the tube, and second, the end of the pen blank will be squared up to the barrel.

Use a pen vise to firmly hold the blank in place. (For picture purposes, the pen blank is held firmly with one hand in Figure 14.) A portable hand drill with a barrel trimmer attached is used to square the end of the tube. If completed properly, the end of the tube will be slightly shiny as shown in Figure 15. Use caution not to remove too much of the tube. If too much of the tube is removed the pen will not assemble properly. Complete the trimming for all the other ends of the tubes. (See Figure 15.) Take care not to be too aggressive while using the barrel trimmer. If you use too much force or go too fast with the drill you may split the wood apart.

A disc sander may also be used to square the end of the tube. Make sure that your pen blank is at an exact 90 degree angle to the head of the sander. Again, use caution not to sand away too much of the brass tube. If you do sand away too much of the tube, the pieces of your pen may not fit together properly.

Mounting your pen blank

Insert a mandrel long enough to hold both the upper and lower portions of the pen blank into the headstock of your lathe. Place the "squared up" pen blank on the mandrel with the appropriate bushings for the pen kit you chose. (The bushings will guide you as you remove wood from the blank. Once the turned wood and the bushings are level, the pen has been turned to size.) Double check that you have your pen blank oriented properly. In other words, make sure that the upper portion of the pen blank and the lower portion of the pen blank are situated on the mandrel correctly.

Screw the locking nut onto the end of the mandrel making sure that it is not put on too tightly. If the locking nut is placed on too tightly, you may damage the mandrel and create a pen that is not round. Snug the tail stock up into the mandrel and again make sure that it is not too tight. The pen blank is now ready to be turned.

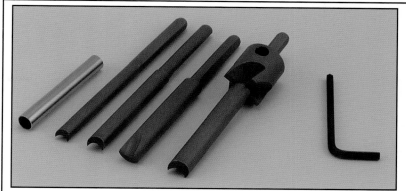

Figure 13: This photo shows a set of barrel-trimming tools ranging in size from 7mm to 10mm.

Figure 14: To show how a barrel trimmer works, this photo was taken with a pen blank held in one hand and the drill in the other. Always use a clamp—not your fingers—to hold a blank during drilling.

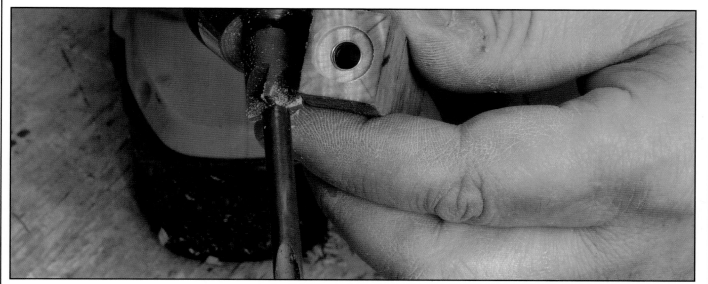

Figure 15: After the barrel trimmer has finished its job, the pen tube is clean, the excess wood has been removed and the pen blank is now square. The next step is turning.

Chapter Four
Pen Turning Tool Techniques

The ABC's of tool control

The **"A" stands for anchor.** Make sure that your turning tool is *firmly* placed on the tool rest *before* contact is made with the pen blank. I know of no better way to catch a turner's immediate and undivided attention than seeing, hearing and feeling a turning tool making contact with the material before the tool is firmly placed on the tool rest. Failing to secure the tool upon the tool rest prior to making contact with the wood will have a detrimental effect on you and possibly your pen blank.

The **"B" stands for bevel.** Confirm that only the bevel touches the surface of the material before you start your cutting. If this does not occur, you will get an immediate "dig-in" and once again possibly ruin your pen blank.

The **"C" stands for cut.** Once the tool is anchored and only the bevel of the tool is touching the surface of the material, can you now slowly raise the handle of the tool to engage the surface of the material and proceed with your cut.

The "ABC's" described above outline a procedure known as bevel cutting. You will obtain a dramatically smoother and better cut by letting the bevel rub against the surface of the material rather than by "scraping" the material. Remember to put these principles into practice as viewed in the next few pages.

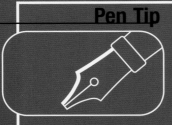

Speed of the lathe

Almost all pen blanks can be prepared with the speed of the lathe set between 1800 and 2000 rpm. For pen blanks that are very large or irregularly shaped, such as blanks made from deer antler, you'll want to slow the lathe speed down to approximately 600 to 800 rpm until the blank is rounded. Once the blank is rounded the lathe speed can be increased to the higher speed listed above with no adverse effect on either you or the pen blank.

Position the tool rest

Place the prepared pen blank on the mandrel with the bushings that are appropriate for the pen you are planning to turn. Assure that your pen blank is properly oriented on the mandrel as indicated by the marks you made when you first cut your pen blank. (See Figure 1.) Adjust the tool rest height to approximately the center of the pen blank as shown. It is important not to have the tool rest too high or too low with respect to the material you will be turning. If this occurs, the possibility of damaging your work is above average.

Rotate the hand wheel brake to make sure that the pen blank will not hit the tool rest. (See Figure 2.) If the blank does strike the tool rest, adjust the tool rest so you have approximately ⅛" space in between the pen blank and your tool rest. You do not want a large gap between the tool rest and your pen blank. A large gap increases your chances of jamming the turning tool between the tool rest and the pen blank causing a serious catch or worse, serious damage to the pen and the tool. (See Figure 3.)

Tool holding techniques

There are two ways to hold the turning tool. The first is the "underhand" technique of holding the tool. Note the position of the thumb. (See Figure 4.) It lightly holds down the top of the tool while your fingers support the tool from the bottom. Meanwhile, your other hand holds the back of the tool, waiting until you slowly raise the tool in order to make contact with the pen blank and start your cutting action. This technique can be done with either your left or your right hand.

The second way to hold a turning tool is called the "overhand" technique. (See Figure 5.) The hand in the foreground is firmly holding the tool down on against the tool rest while the back hand is holding the tool, waiting to raise the tool up in order to make

Figure 1: Following the directions in the pen kit you purchased, orient the blank and the bushings on the mandrel.

Figure 2: Turn the pen blank to ensure that the tool rest does not touch the pen blank.

contact with the material.

This overhand technique is primarily used for turning larger objects, while the underhand technique is most widely used for turning pens and other smaller objects.

Figure 3: If the tool rest is too far from the pen blank, the tool may catch between the blank and the rest.

Figure 4: In the underhand grip, the forefingers ride on the rest and the thumb applies slight pressure downward on the roughing gouge.

Figure 5: The overhand tool grip is usually used when you are roughing out larger pieces.

Tools of the trade

Roughing Gouge

The first tool you will use to turn a pen will be a roughing gouge. (See Figures 6, 7 and 8.) This tool is used to cut away the square stock of your blank and turn it into a round cylinder. Again, note the position of the hand holding the roughing gouge; this is the "underhand" technique of holding the tool.

The roughing gouge is best utilized by placing the gouge firmly on the tool rest, part A of the turning ABC's. Then advance the heel of the tool, which is the lower portion of the bevel, to come in contact with the wood, which is part B. As the bevel of the gouge starts to make contact with the wood, slowly start to raise the handle of the tool, engaging the wood to obtain a clean cut on the surface of the material, which covers part C.

Spindlemaster

This unique tool is a cross between a skew and a spindle gouge. Its best advantage is that it takes the fear of using a skew out of the hands of the beginner. It can take the place of both a spindle gouge and a skew chisel. (See Figures 9 and 10.)

Place the Spindlemaster firmly on the tool rest before engaging it with the wood – A. Let the bevel come in contact with the surface – B. Slowly raise the handle of the tool to start cutting the material – C. Note how clean the surface becomes when the correct bevel rubbing technique is applied. When the correct cut is attained, you will achieve shavings similar to the ones shown.

Parting tool

The parting tool has many uses for general turning as well as specific uses for pen turning. (See Figures 11 and 12.) The parting tool should be held at a right angle to the surface you are cutting when you are using it in the bevel rubbing mode as shown on the opposite page. Note that the parting tool is anchored on the tool rest—A, the bevel of the tool is touching the pen blank—B, and when the handle of the tool is slowly raised, the cutting will commence—C. When properly completed, the parting tool will cut a clean tenon.

Spindle gouge, ¼"

Some turners like to put a bead or cove into some of their pens, while others do not. If you are going to turn any small objects other than pens, a small spindle gouge is a must. (See Figure 13.) Again, start as before with the gouge resting on the tool rest. Now advance the gouge into the work so just the heel of the bevel is slightly rubbing against the

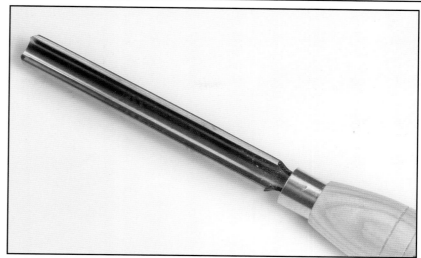

Figure 6: A roughing gouge is the first tool used when turning a pen. It removes the square corners of the blank.

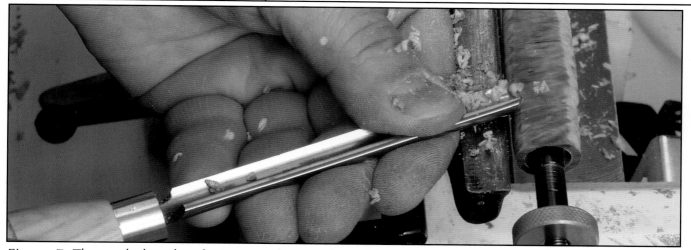

Figure 7: The underhand technique and a roughing gouge are used here to remove the corners of the blank.

Figure 8: A roughing gouge and the bevel rubbing technique, side-to-side motion that removes surface wood, is used here to round the blank.

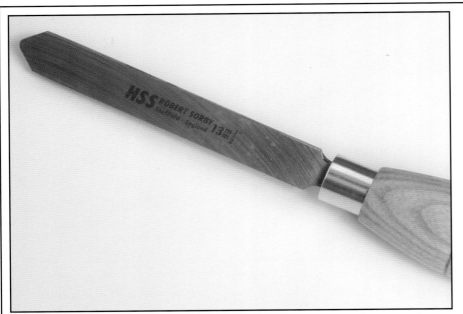

Figure 9: The spindlemaster is a cross between a skew and a spindle gouge.

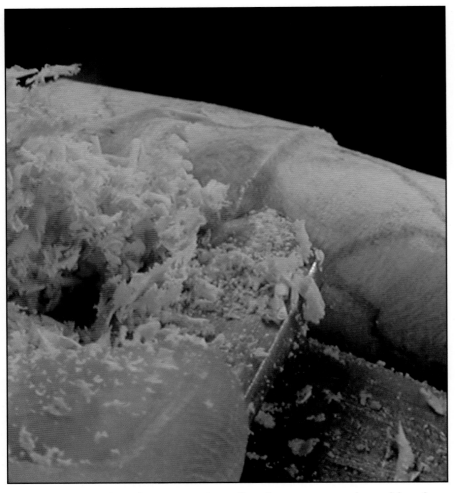

Figure 10: Notice the exceptionally clean cut produced by the spindlemaster.

work. Now, slowly start to raise the handle of the gouge and roll the tool to the right. The flute of the tool should be facing away from the bead when finished. Do the same procedure to the opposite side to create a perfect bead.

Skew chisel

This tool strikes fear into the hearts of most turners who are just starting to learn the art of turning. (See Figures 14 and 15.) However, once you learn to properly use the skew it will be your new best friend! Start by anchoring the skew on the tool rest – A. Slowly advance the skew until the bevel touches the surface of your material – B. Gently and slowly lift the handle of the skew until the center of the skew starts to cut the surface of the pen blank – C. If you do not present the bevel of the skew to pen blank properly, the results will be the dreaded "dig-in."

When you master the skew, you will be cutting with the center of the tool or the "sweet spot." The sweet spot on the skew is located in the center of the skew between the "toe," the upper portion, and the lower portion of the skew, the "heel." When the tool is properly used, you will be rewarded with a superior finishing cut and with shavings as shown.

Sandpaper

While sandpaper is not technically a tool, it can remove quite a bit of wood during the final stages of pen turning. That's why, as you'll see later, I suggest that you don't turn a pen all the way down to the bushings before sanding. If you do, the sanding process may remove too much wood, making the wood of the pen lower than the bushings, and creating a pen that won't assemble properly.

Most beginners will start sanding with 150 grit paper. Because the

Spindlemaster makes a fine finish cut, starting with 220 grit sandpaper is possible. With practice using a skew, an even better finishing cut may be obtained thus allowing you to start with an even higher grit sandpaper.

The sanding steps for beginners are as follows: 150 grit, 180 grit, 220 grit, 320 grit and 400 grit. Sand lightly. Too much pressure will cause excessive heat, which will crack the pen. The 400 grit sandpaper will give a great finish. I usually take my pens to 1500 grit and even higher. I have found that the extra time—maybe one minute—that it takes to sand to this level is very small in comparison with getting a surface that has no micro scratches.

As you add turning tools to your toolbox, remember to follow the ABC's of tool control and you will be rewarded with many enjoyable hours of smooth, controlled cuts that turn beautiful pens.

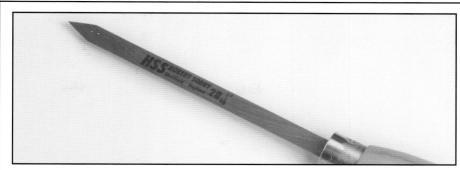

Figure 11: A parting tool is a useful tool for special cuts.

Figure 12: Here a parting tool is used to cut a tenon on a blank.

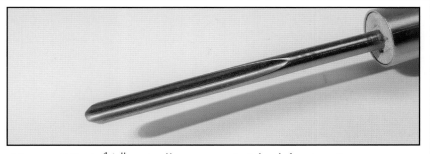

Figure 13: A $1/4''$ spindle gouge is ideal for turning decorative beads and coves in your pens.

Figure 14: A skew chisel, which can be an aggressive tool, is an important tool in a pen turner's toolbox.

Figure 15: Note the clean shavings you can obtain using the sweet spot of a skew chisel.

Chapter Five
Dyeing/Staining Wood

For hundreds of years, a desirable finishing technique for furniture makers has been to change the color of the wood while allowing the grain patterns to be a visual part of their creations. It seems a sacrilege to take a highly figured, beautiful piece of tiger striped or bird's eye maple and artificially inject another color into the grain pattern, but that is exactly what will be accomplished in the following section. And the results are stunning.

Many different companies produce good quality dyes and stains for wood. You must choose a stain that is correct for your particular application. For pen turning, a stain should be fade resistant, include ultraviolet protection and dry quickly. Most importantly, the stain should not raise the grain. This is important because stain is applied after the pen blank has been thoroughly sanded.

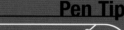

Aniline Dyes

Most turners are familiar with aniline dyes. Aniline dyes are fine powders that have to be dissolved in water, alcohol or other solvents depending on the formula that is chosen. Water-soluble aniline dyes are good for transparency of color and are easy to apply. The drawback with water-soluble dyes is that they may raise the grain, giving a fuzzy appearance to your project. The "fuzzies" can be removed, but this is another step to complete. An alternative to the aniline dyes is alcohol-based stains.

Alcohol-based stains

Non-grain-raising (NGR) dyes are alcohol-based dyes. Solar-Lux by Behlen is an NGR dye that is UV resistant. These dyes are used for several reasons: The stains that are offered can be used directly from the bottle, the stains may be mixed with each other to create other colors, and the translucency will enhance the pen blank's grain patterns. In other words, they are easy to mix and apply, and they create unique grain patterns.

A Word of Caution About Dyes

Avoid absorbing the dye through your skin. Wear gloves when working with dyes. Dyes will stain your hands if protection is not worn. Make sure adequate ventilation is present and wear a mask. To avoid the possibility of spontaneous combustion, discard the application rag outside in a metal container. Check with your local municipality regarding the proper disposal of such materials.

Dyeing the Pen Blank

Move the tool rest out of the way and thoroughly sand the pen

Non-grain-raising stain, such as Solarlux, is used to add color to your pen.

Here I am applying raw sienna with a piece of cheese cloth. Note the glove worn to protect my hand from the stain.

blank to at least 600 grit or higher. Completely remove any dust that is present on the pen blank. If compressed air is available, use this to clean the pen blank.

Do not fill the grain or seal the wood. The stain must be able to penetrate the wood fibers.

The pen in this example will be dyed yellow. Wearing protective gloves pour a small amount of raw sienna (yellow) stain directly from the bottle onto a piece of cheesecloth. While the pen blank is turning, lightly apply the stain to the pen blank. Make sure the blank is covered thoroughly.

Complete both halves of the blank. Application of the stain should take no more than 15-20 seconds for both halves. Immediately, place a small amount of Triple EEE cream on a clean piece of cheese cloth and remove the excess stain from the wood. Continue to use the EEE cream for about 30-45 seconds.

After the Triple EEE cream is applied, use the woodturner's finish on a paper towel and lightly apply the finish. Note how shiny the wood is and how much the grain stands out.

The stain has been applied full strength.

I remove the excess stain with EEE polish and a piece of cheese cloth.

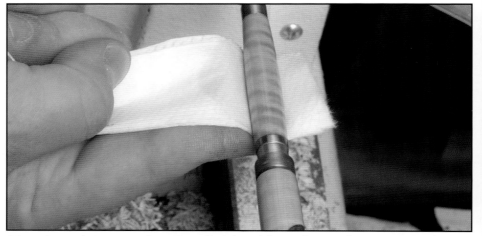

Next I apply a woodturning finish with a piece of paper towel.

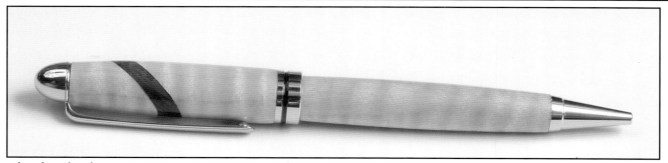

The finished pen. Raw sienna penetrated and enhanced the grain of the tiger-striped maple. The dark stripe was cut from cocobolo.

Part Two
Turning Wooden Pens

Now that you know the basics of pen turning, it is time to put your knowledge to the ultimate test: turning a pen in wood. In this section you will learn step-by-step how to turn a Slimline pen from a wooden blank. The step-by-step section is followed by five additional pen-turning projects that can be done in any type of wood. Remember to think small when choosing interesting wood for your blanks and to follow the ABC's of turning as you proceed.

Project One
The Slimline Pen

The Slimline pen will use a standard 7mm mandrel, 7mm bushings and a 7mm drill bit. The plain band used in the demonstration can be switched out for a more ornate band as shown above. The blank for this pen was cut from a maple burl growing in the forests of Virginia.

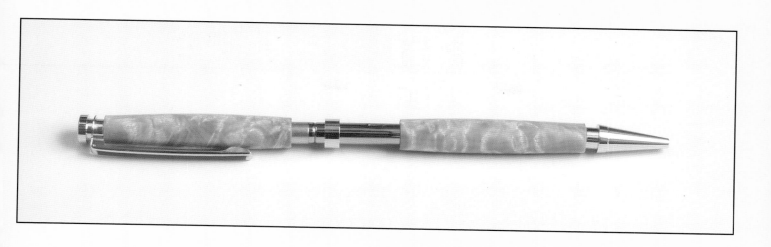

Prepare the Pen Blank

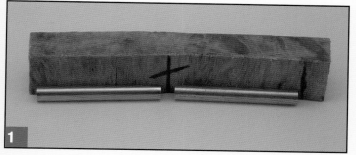

Note that the pen blank, cut from a maple burl, may not be the best looking or the straightest; however, it still will make an excellent pen because of the figure in the wood. Mark the pen blank to size by using the pen tubes as a guide. Note the orientation marks on the blank and add an extra 1⁄16" minimum on each end of the blank to allow for drilling.

Find the center of each piece of the blank by drawing a line from corner to corner as shown.

Place the pen blank into the pen vise and drill the blank using a brad point drill bit. Relieve the blank often to remove chips and avoid heat build-up, which could cause the end of the pen blank to blow out.

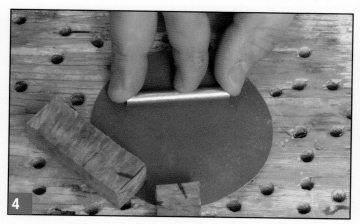

Rough up the tubes by rubbing them against a piece of 100-grit sandpaper.

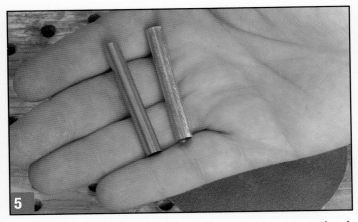

Note that the tube on the right has been roughed up and the tube on the left has not.

Use thin cyanoacrylate (CA) glue to coat the inside of the pen blank.

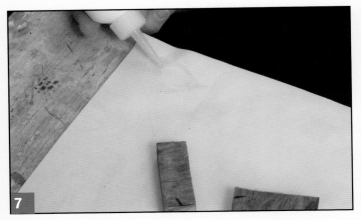

Place a small amount of medium CA glue on waxed paper.

Place the pen tube on the insertion tool and cover the tube in the medium CA glue to coat the outside of tube.

Insert the tube into one end of the pen blank and move it in and out to coat one half of the inside of the blank.

Remove the tube and roll it in medium CA glue again. Reinsert it into the other end of the pen blank, and move it in and out again to coat the other half of the inside of the pen blank.

When the insides of both halves of the blank are covered with glue insert the tube to just inside the end of the pen blank as shown.

Note how the end is square with the pen blank and the brass tube.

Using a roughing gouge in the bevel rubbing technique, start with the gouge lightly touching the pen blank. Move it back and forth along the blank to start the rounding process.

Square the ends of pen blank using a pen mill. The pen mill can be attached to a portable drill or it can be used by hand. (The pen vised was omitted for photographic purposes.)

Turning the Slimline Pen

Position the mandrel into the headstock of the lathe and then place the pen blanks on the mandrel with the correct bushings (7mm) for the Slimline pen. Note the orientation marks on the pen blank. Thread the lock nut on the mandrel so it's tight, but do not over-tighten it.

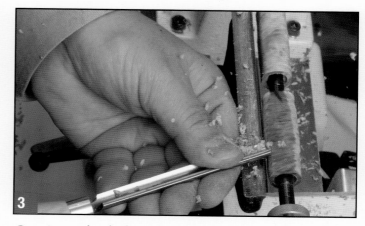

Continue the light rubbing process as more chips start to fly.

As the blank becomes more round, apply slightly more pressure with your back hand to cut more wood.

Continue this process and start to add some shape to your pen at this time.

At this point you'll need to adjust your tool rest to keep it approximately ⅛" from your pen blank.

After the blanks are approximately the same size you can now use the Spindlemaster to start the final shaping of the pen. Note the clean finish that can achieved by the bevel rubbing technique used in the previous steps. Also notice the shavings that are coming off the Spindlemaster.

As I mentioned before, you can use either hand to turn your pen. Here the author uses his left hand to cut the shape of the pen.

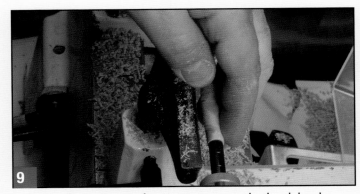

Word of caution: If you must touch the blank while it is running, touch it on the top or slightly in front as illustrated. Do not touch the moving blank on the side nearest to you, because your finger will get caught between the tool rest and the moving piece.

Sanding the Pen Blank

Before you begin to sand the pen blank, take note of these few items. First, the sandpaper is coming in contact with the pen on the bottom of the blank at approximately the 7 o'clock position. Second, there is adequate suction being generated by the dust collection system to draw the dust being produced by the sanding of the pen blank into the dust hood. Make sure that you are wearing your dust mask. Third, the tool rest has been moved aside to facilitate the sanding process.

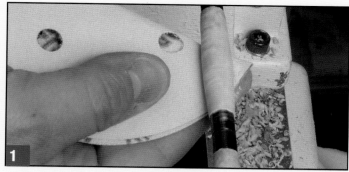

Once you have the desired shape, leave the blank slightly proud of the bushings. In other words do not make the pen blank flush with the bushings at this time. If you do, when you sand the blank, the wood for the pen will be lower than the bushings and a good fit will not be possible.

When you feel you have a smooth transition between the bushings and blank then stop. Here you can see that the blank and the bushing are equal, assuring a good transition between the pen tip and the blank.

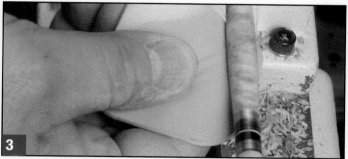

The sanding steps for beginners are: 150 grit, 180 grit, 220 grit, 320 grit and 400 grit. Sand lightly. Too much pressure will cause excessive heat, which will crack the pen. 400-grit sandpaper will give a great finish. This author takes his pens to 4000 grit and even higher. Notice the shine on the blank with no finish on it yet!

Applying a Finish

The first question my students ask about finishing is what products they should use. There are tons of finishing products on the market today. After trying many different products and procedures, I have boiled finishing down to the following few simple, but effective steps.

The second question students always ask is how many coats of finish to apply. My answer is that since the pen is turning at 1800 rpm's, then in theory you are applying 1800 mini coats of finish per minute! However, putting one solid coat of finish on the pen has always been sufficient for my customers, and after all, that is the ultimate test!

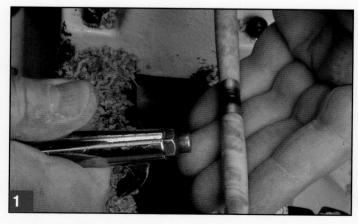

Use compressed air to blow off any dust that is left after the sanding process.

First, use a small amount of Triple EEE cream on a piece of cheese cloth.

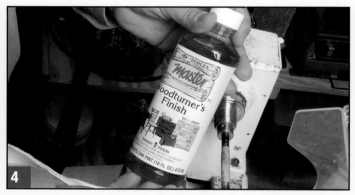

Next, pour woodturner's finish onto a piece of paper towel and apply light pressure to the bottom of the blank, moving it back and forth very slowly. As the finish starts to dry slowly start to put more pressure on the blank. The blank will become warm as the friction seals in the shine.

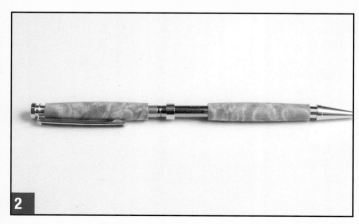

Line up the parts on the pen blanks as shown per the instructions in your pen kit.

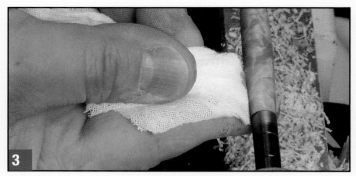

Rub it back and forth on the bottom edge of your blank. Note how the part of the pen blank in the foreground where the EEE cream was applied is brighter than the part of the pen in the background where the Triple EEE has not touched. As you are moving back and forth, a slight amount of heat is being generated. This is normal.

Assembling the Pen

Remove the blanks from the mandrel taking caution to keep them in the same orientation that you turned them and place them aside for assembly on the assembly rack.

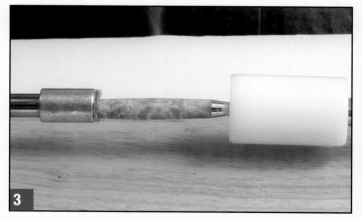

Start with the tip of the pen and press it into the front end of the blank.

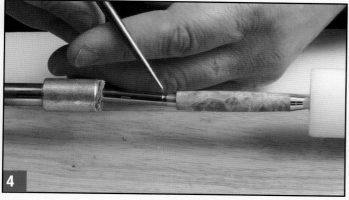

Press the twist mechanism into the pen to the mark on the line. Also note that the mechanism should *not* be going in on an angle as shown. The severe angle may cause the end of the pen to split!

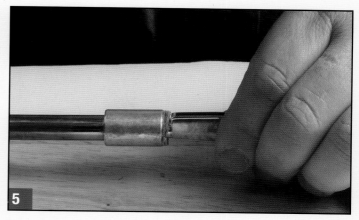

Next press the top cap and clip into the top tube.

Place the band over the twist mechanism and push the top section into the bottom section.

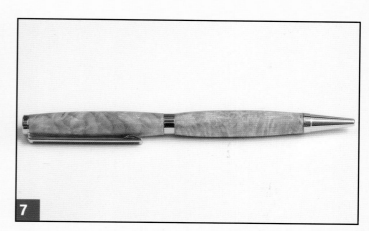

Here is your finished pen – Congratulations!

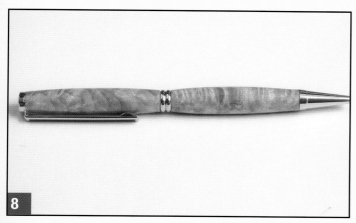

If you want a little variation, try putting a different center band on your pen.

Project Two
Box Elder Comfort Pen

The popularity of the Comfort pen makes this an admired style of pen and gives it an excellent track record for sales at craft fairs and shows. Shown here is a Comfort pen turned from a piece of box elder. The standard 7mm mandrel is used in conjunction with the Comfort bushing set. Use two standard 7mm bushings then the Comfort bushing, followed by the lower blank, another comfort bushing, the upper blank and a 7mm bushing.

Pen Tip

• Do not remove more than 1" of wood from the lower bushing or the comfort grip will be loose.

• When squaring the ends of the pen blanks, do not remove more of the brass tube than is necessary.

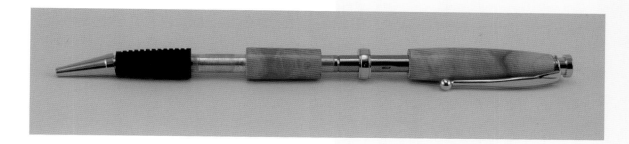

1. Cut the pen blank to the proper length and add ¹⁄₁₆" on each end.

2. Rough up the pen tubes by rubbing them on a piece of 100 grit sandpaper.

3. Drill the blank using a drill press and a 7mm brad point drill bit.

4. Glue the pen tubes into the blanks using thin CA glue followed by medium CA glue. Use a twisting motion to spread the glue evenly inside the pen blank.

5. A 7mm barrel trimmer is used to square the ends of the blanks 90° flush to the ends of the brass tubes.

6. Insert the mandrel into the headstock of the lathe and then place two 7mm spacer bushings on the mandrel. Now place a Comfort bushing and the lower pen blank. Next place a second Comfort bushing, then upper blank followed by a 7mm bushing and the locking nut.

7. Use the roughing gouge to start turning your pen. Continue to reduce the blanks using either the spindlemaster or the skew to give the blanks the final shape just slightly proud of the bushings.

8. Because the Comfort pen uses the gripper collar on the lower portion of the pen, measure 1" from the end of the lower barrel and use the parting tool in the bevel rubbing mode as demonstrated to cut a clean shoulder.

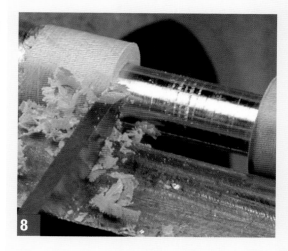

9. Move the tool rest out of the way and start sanding to a desired finish. I recommend at least to 800 grit. Apply the aluminum 2400, 4000 grit oxide pads (dry) using a light touch to obtain a micro fine shine.

10. Apply woodturner's finish with a paper towel to the finished blanks.

11. Line up all the parts according to the instructions in the Comfort pen kit and assemble your pen.

Project Three
Bird's Eye Maple Roller Ball Pen

Roller ball pens come in two general sizes: "Classic Elite" and the standard "Classic Roller Ball" pen. The main difference between the two styles is the size. The Classic Elite is a smaller pen and will fit into a pocket or purse with room to spare. In addition, the Classic Elite uses a gel roller ball. The pen shown here is the Classic Elite Roller Ball pen. The steps to make the Classic Elite and the Classic Roller Ball pens are identical; the only differences are in the size of the pen and the type of roller ball.

Pen Tip

• Care should be used when removing wood for the center band.

• When not in use, keep the cap on the pen to extend the life of the gel roller ball.

Both pens are made from bird's eye curly maple; however, the bottom pen has been stained. Note how the stain makes the grain stand out.

1. Cut the pen blank to the proper length and add ¹⁄₁₆" on each end. Then rough up the pen tubes by rubbing them on a piece of 100-grit sandpaper.

2. Drill the blank using a drill press and a 7mm brad point drill bit. Glue the pen tubes into the blanks first using thin CA glue followed by medium CA glue. Use a twisting motion to spread the glue evenly inside the pen blank.

3. A 7mm barrel trimmer is used to square the ends of the blanks 90° flush to the ends of the brass tubes.

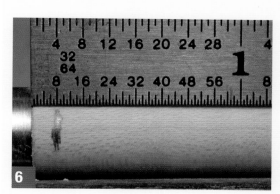

4. Insert the mandrel into the headstock of the lathe. Place a standard 7mm bushing and the lower cap bushing. Next place the lower blank, then the center bushing, the upper blank, the upper cap bushing and another 7mm spacer bushing.

5. Use the roughing gouge to start turning your pen. Continue to reduce the blanks using the skew, assuring that the blank is straight across and just slightly proud of the bushings.

6. Wood needs to be removed from the upper cap to accommodate the center bushing. Measure ¹⁄₈" from the end of the center bushing.

7. Using a parting tool, remove the ¹⁄₈" from the top barrel of the pen.

8. Use a straight edge to assure that the blank is straight across.

9. Move the tool rest out of the way and start sanding to the desired finish. I recommend at least 800 grit. Apply the aluminum 2400 and 4000 grit oxide pads (dry) using a light touch to obtain a micro-fine shine.

10. Apply woodturner's finish to the turned pen blanks.

11. Line up all the parts according to the instructions in the Classic Elite pen kit and assemble your pen.

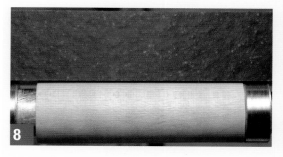

Project Four
Maple Burl Click Pen

The "ole click pen" makes a comeback. This is a first cousin to the Slimline pen, but it is a much more robust pen. It incorporates a "Parker" style gel ink refill with a serious click mechanism. This pen sold out at the first craft fair that it was displayed and many more have been made since that time. The gel refill makes the pen very smooth when writing, and the extra girth makes it popular with people who need a larger pen. Use the standard 7mm mandrel in conjunction with the Slimline-Pro three-piece bushing set. The drill bit used in this demonstration is an 8mm brad point drill bit.

Pen Tip

* Relieve debris often during drilling to avoid the dreaded "blowout" at the bottom of the pen blank.

* Use a light touch when sanding to avoid excessive heat build up and the resultant cracking of the pen blank.

1. Measure the pen blank to the proper length and add ⅟₁₆" on each end. Cut the blanks, then rough up the pen tubes by rubbing them on a piece of 100-grit sandpaper.

2. Drill the blank using a drill press and an 8mm brad point drill bit.

3. Glue the pen tubes into the blanks first using thin CA glue followed by medium CA glue. Use a twisting motion to spread the glue evenly inside the pen blank.

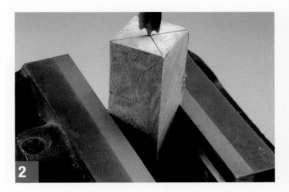

4. An 8mm barrel trimmer is used to square the ends of the blanks 90° flush to the ends of the brass tubes.

5. Insert the mandrel into the headstock of the lathe and use the Slimline-Pro bushings.

6. Use the roughing gouge to start turning your pen and continue to reduce the blanks using a skew to get a smooth finish as illustrated.

7. Move the tool rest out of the way and start sanding to a desired finish. I recommend at least to 800 grit. When finished, use a straight edge and place it on top of the blank to make sure that it is straight across.

8. Apply woodturner's finish with a paper towel to the turned blanks.

9. Assemble your pen according to the instructions in the Slimline-Pro kit.

Project Five
Lacewood Cigar Pen

These big, beefy, well-built pens are always a favorite at shows and craft fairs. Designed with strength and power in mind, the pen still fits in your hand with elegance and grace. This is a preferred pen for people who want to make a statement with their writing instrument. These pens are always a top seller with people who have a problem holding a smaller pen. Use the standard 7mm mandrel in conjunction with the cigar three-piece bushing set. The drill bit used in this demonstration is a 10mm brad point drill bit.

Pen Tip

• Turn the hand wheel before starting the lathe to assure that the pen blank will not hit the tool rest.

• Adjust tool rest height to approximately the mid-line of the pen and make sure it is always about 1/8" away from the pen blank.

1. Cut the pen blank to the proper length and add ¹⁄₁₆" on each end. Then rough up the pen tubes by rubbing them on a piece of 100-grit sandpaper.

2. Drill the blank using a drill press and an 10mm brad point drill bit.

3. Glue the pen tubes into the blanks first using thin CA glue followed by medium CA glue. Use a twisting motion to spread the glue evenly inside the pen blank.

4. An 10mm barrel trimmer is used to square the ends of the blanks 90° flush to the ends of the brass tubes.

5. Insert the mandrel into the headstock of the lathe and use the cigar bushings as illustrated. Note that the blank will hit the tool rest if the lathe is turned on at this point. Check to be sure the blank is clear before starting your lathe.

6. Use the roughing gouge to start turning your pen. Continue to reduce the blanks using the skew or spindlemaster. The top barrel should have a slight taper toward the cap bushing.

7. Move the tool rest out of the way and start sanding to a desired finish. I recommend sanding to at least 800 grit.

8. Use woodturner's finish on the turned blanks.

9. Assemble your pen according to the instructions in the Cigar Pen kit.

Eurostyle Pens: The blank for the pen on the left is made with the grain running parallel to blank. The blank for the pen on the right was cut at a 15 degree angle. Both pens are made from cocobolo.

A trilogy of zebrawood pens. The blank for the pen on the left was cut at a 15 degree angle. The pen in the middle was turned with the end grain. The blank for the pen on the right was cut with the grain running parallel.

Dyed Pens (from left to right): Eurostyle, curly maple, blue; Eurostyle, curly maple, mahogany; Eurostyle, bird's eye maple, mahogany; Classic Elite roller ball, curly maple, red; Classic Elite roller ball, curly maple, red and mahogany; Eurostyle, curly maple with cocobolo stripe, raw sienna.

Wood Pens (left to right): Eurostyle, spalted maple turned cross-grain; Eurostyle, spalted maple, turned parallel to the grain.

Part Three
Turning Pens from Other Materials

In addition to wood, there are a number of materials that can be turned on a mini-lathe. Any one of these materials can be made into an interesting and unique pen. In the following section, you'll learn step-by-step how to turn a cigar style pen from Corian®, a solid surface substance most often used in kitchen and vanity countertops. Five other projects, each using a different material—everything from acrylics to deer antler—follow the main demonstration.

Project One
Cigar Pen
Corian®

The cigar pen uses a 10mm drill bit, 10mm bushings, and a standard 7mm mandrel.

Pen Tip

• **Keep your tools sharp. This is especially important when turning solid surface materials.**

• **Glue the "good sides" of the blanks together so the seam does not show.**

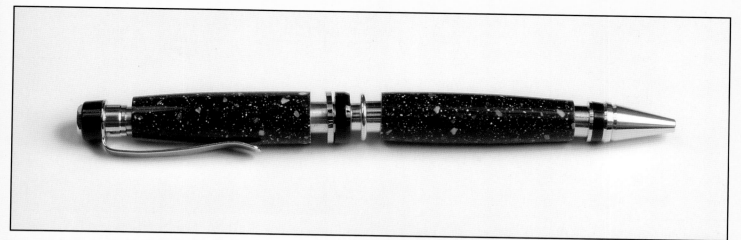

Prepare the Corian® Pen Blank

Turning Corian is just as easy to turn as wood. When turning Corian it is especially important that you start out with sharpened tools and keep them sharp throughout the turning process.

Corian comes in three different thicknesses. For our purposes of pen making, the ½" size will serve our needs best because of the wide variety of colors offered. However, since most of the larger pens need a thicker pen blank of at least ⅝" to ¾", the ½" material must be glued together to form a larger pen blank.

The first step will be to glue two pieces of Corian together so the glue line does not show after it is turned. There is nothing more frustrating than gluing pieces together, turning the blank and then noticing that you can see the glue line. The method that follows will ensure that your glue lines will not be visible.

Corian has a good side, which is smoother than the back side. The back side may have writing on it. Cut two pieces of Corian ¾" x ¾" x 5¼". Wipe the good sides with ethyl alcohol and allow them to dry.

Place the pen tubes on the pen blank and add ¹⁄₁₆" to each end for proper length. Do not forget to mark which blank is the upper (short) blank and which is the lower (long) blank.

Coat the facing sides with medium thickness CA glue and clamp them together (Note that one clamp was removed for picture clarity.) Spray accelerator will speed up the drying process; however, wait at least 15 minutes for the glue to thoroughly cure.

4

Cut the pen blank to the proper length. Use the pen tubes as a guide as shown.

Drilling and Gluing the Pen Tubes

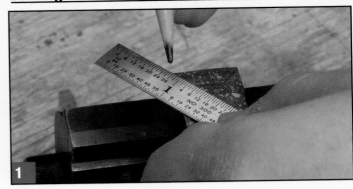

1

Place the cut pen blank into the pen vise and draw a diagonal line from corner to corner to find the exact center of the blank.

2

Use a small square to make sure that the pen blank is perpendicular to the drill bit.

3

Drill the blank using a drill press and a high-speed steel twist drill bit. The secret to drilling acrylic material is to make sure that you frequently remove drilled material from the blank.

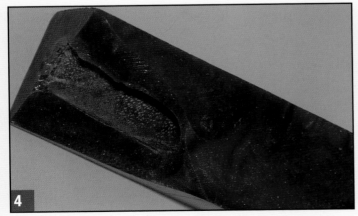

4

As you get toward the end of the pen blank, lighten your touch on the drill so you will not have a blowout at the end. Blowouts are the result of too much heat building up because you are going too fast.

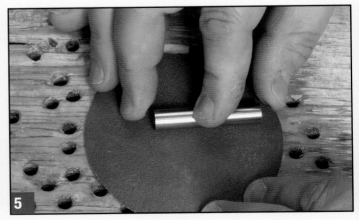

5

Scratch the surface of the pen tubes using a piece of 100-grit sandpaper. Scratching the surface will make the glue bond better with the surface.

The Pen Turner's Workbook

Notice the tube on the left is for the lower blank. It is not scratched. The tube on the right is for the upper blank. That one has been scratched.

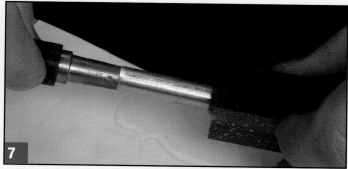

Glue the scratched tubes inside the drilled blanks. Place the longer tube on the insertion tool and roll the tube in CA glue. Place the tube into one end of the blank, rolling it around and going in and out of the hole. Repeat the same motion on the other end of the blank and insert the tube. Let dry for 15 minutes.

Place the 10mm barrel trimming tool into a drill. Slowly start to square up the ends of the tube so they are even with the end of the blank. The barrel trimming tool will clean any CA glue from the inside of the tube. Use the pen vise to hold the pen blank while squaring the tube. It is being held here by hand for picture purposes only.

Trim the pen only to the end of the brass. If you trim too much of the blank away, the pieces will not fit together properly when you assemble the pen.

Turning the Corian Pen Blanks

First, place a 7mm spacer bushing on the mandrel. The front 10mm bushing followed by the lower blank, then the center bushing, then the upper blank, and finally the top 10mm bushing and a 7mm spacer bushing. Note the size difference between the 7mm bushing on the right and the 10mm bushing on the left.

Insert the mandrel into the headstock of the lathe. Place the 10mm bushings on the mandrel with the smaller bushing in the front, followed by the center bushing, then the larger top bushing as shown.

Move the tool rest up and center it, leaving approximately ⅛" between the tool rest and the pen blanks. Rotate the hand wheel to make sure that the blanks do not come in contact with the tool rest.

Using the roughing gouge in the bevel rubbing mode start to lightly rub against the blank, taking off little bits of the Corian at a time. Note the shavings coming off the blank.

Check for roundness of the blank by placing the gouge on top of the blank as shown. If you hear a "rap, rap, rap" sound you know you still have to turn some more to make it round.

Continue to round over the blank. As you get the blank to a more rounded state, you will get longer streams of material coming off your gouge.

Remember, as the blank continues to get smaller you must keep moving the tool rest closer to the blank. Now you can start to apply more pressure on your tool and take deeper cuts in order to remove more material faster.

Once the blanks are round, the spindlemaster can be used to start to shape the pen.

Notice the clean shavings from this tool and how the left hand is being used to turn the blank. Do not be afraid to use both hands. Once you learn to use your non-dominant hand you will become a better turner.

Use a skew on the lower blank to clean up the blank up and to give it the final shape you want. As with the wooden pen, leave the blank slightly proud of the bushings so you can sand it flush.

As you get toward the desired shape, use a skew chisel to clean up the ends of the blank. Note how the sweet spot of the skew is used, and look at the fine shavings being generated.

Sanding and Finishing Your Corian® Pen

A quick note about sanding acrylic material... Padded aluminum oxide sanding pads have been used by the kitchen and bath industry for years to take away scratches on the counter top surfaces. Because we are using the same material, Corian, why shouldn't we use this same technology to polish our pens to a scratch-free shine? The brightly colored aluminum oxide sanding pads can be quickly used to sand and polish your pen to a scratch-free shine. Use each successive pad for the same amount of time. Usually this is about 10-15 seconds per sanding pad.

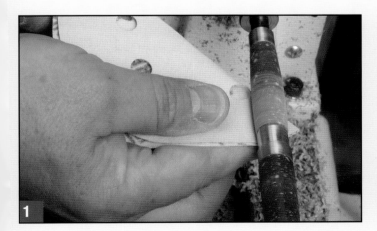

Move the tool rest out of the way and sand the blank with 220-grit sandpaper until the blank is flush with the bushings.

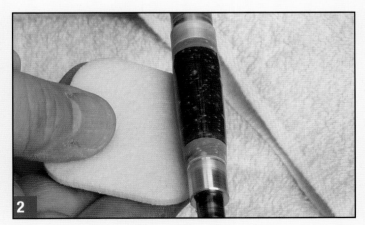

Place a towel on the bed of the lathe to prevent the lathe from becoming wet. Start with the 800 grit 2" x 2" green aluminum oxide pad. Place a few drops of water on the pad and start to wet-sand the blank.

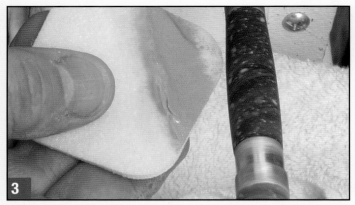

3 There will be a whitish slurry created by the aluminum oxide pads and the Corian surface. This is normal. In reality you are polishing the blank with this slurry. Just wash off the pad and it can be used over and over again.

4 On each half of the blank, use the peach-colored aluminum oxide pad, which is 1500 grit. These pads are used wet with a gentle touch. If too much pressure is applied, the heat generated will cause the glue from the pad to come off on the blank.

5 Purple is the next color used, and it is 2400 grit.

6 Light blue, representing 4000 grit, is the next color. The blanks are becoming shiny, and all the scratches are gone.

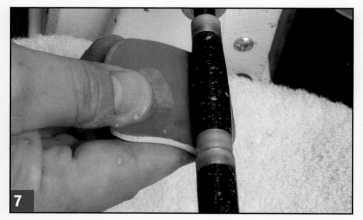

7 The final aluminum oxide sanding pad, gray in color, is 12000 grit. This will feel like nothing, but trust me, it is placing a shine on the material that you will not believe!

8 The entire polishing process starting from the green pad to the gray pad took approximately two minutes—and look at the scratch free shine you have!

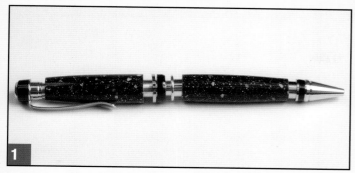

Line up all the parts by placing them into the pen as shown.

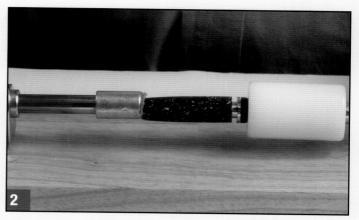

Place the gold disc on the center band. Press the center band into the lower portion of the upper tube.

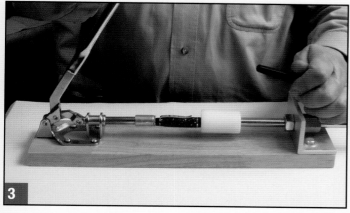

Insert the clip/coupler assembly into the upper portion of the top blank and press them together. The upper portion is complete.

Press the tip into the lower portion of the pen blank with the pen press.

Now press the center coupling into the other end of the lower blank.

Place the refill with the spring inside the lower barrel and screw the twist mechanism on the center coupling. Push the upper portion of the pen on to the lower portion, and now you have the rest of the pen. Do not be alarmed, the twist mechanism will turn both ways to open and close the pen.

Project Two
Comfort Pen
InLace

InLace is an acrylic material that can be easily turned. It offers a wide assortment of colors and styles. It is sold in solid pen blank form and in liquid form to be used to fill in gaps and voids in a variety of turning applications. This pen project will use InLace to make a comfort-style pen.

The Comfort pen is a popular style of pen because of the soft grip collar located on the front of the pen. It is a good seller at shows and in stores. The standard 7mm mandrel will be used in conjunction with a two-piece Comfort bushing set and one standard 7mm bushing. A 7mm high-speed steel drill bit is used to make the pen blank for the Comfort pen.

Pen Tip

• When working with InLace, use a light tool touch. If you apply too much pressure on the pen blank, a very large chip will be taken out of the pen blank.

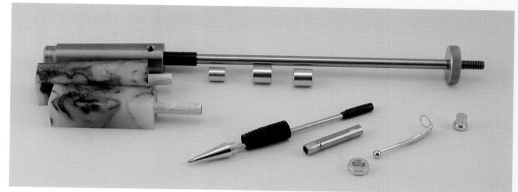

1 Add ⅟₁₆″ to each end and cut the pen blanks to the proper lengths, using the tubes as guides.

2 Rough up the pen tubes with a piece of 100-grit sandpaper. If you are using a light-colored or see-through material, paint the pen tubes a color similar to the pen blank so the brass tube will not show through when the pen is turned.

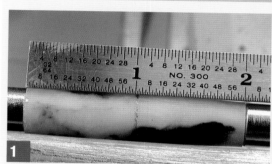

3 Proceed with preparing the pen blank as described in Chapter Three. The secret to drilling acrylic material is to make sure that you relieve the blank often.

4 Use a 7mm barrel trimmer to square the ends of the blanks flush to the ends of the brass tubes.

5 Insert the mandrel into the headstock of the lathe and then place two 7mm spacer bushings on the mandrel. Next add a Comfort bushing, then the lower pen blank, a second Comfort bushing, then upper blank, followed by a 7 mm bushing and the locking nut.

6 Use a roughing gouge to start turning your InLace pen. A word of caution is necessary here: If you try to take too much material, you will damage you pen blank beyond all repair. Take small passes and reduce the blank slowly and carefully.

7 Continue to reduce the pen blanks using either the spindlemaster or the skew to give it the final shape just slightly proud of the bushings.

8 Because the Comfort pen uses the gripper collar on the lower portion of the pen, measure 1″ from the end of the lower barrel. Then use the parting tool in the bevel rubbing mode to pare off the lower portion of the pen blank. The parting tool should cut a clean shoulder.

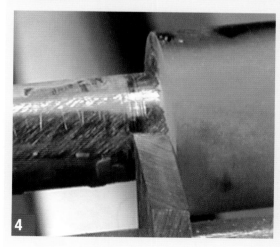

9 Move the tool rest out of the way and start sanding with 220 grit sandpaper. Do not worry about the scratches you see, they will be removed in the next step with the padded aluminum oxide pads.

10 Wet-sand and polish the blanks using the green, peach, purple, light blue and gray aluminum oxide pads.

11 Line up and assemble all the parts according to the instructions in the Comfort pen kit.

Project Three
Euro "Designer" Pen
Polygem

The Euro "Designer" style pen is one of the most popular pens for potential customers to purchase and for pen makers to create. Polygem is another acrylic material that turns very smoothly and offers a different variety of pen blanks for the pen maker.

The standard 7mm mandrel will be used in conjunction with a three piece bushing set.

1 Add ⅟₁₆″ to each end and cut the pen blanks to the proper lengths, using the tubes as guides.

2 Rough up the pen tubes with a piece of 100-grit sandpaper. If you are using a light-colored or see-through material, paint the pen tubes a color similar to the pen blank so the brass tube will not show through when the pen is turned.

3 Proceed with preparing the pen blank as described in Chapter Three. The secret to drilling acrylic material is to make sure that you relieve the blank often.

4 Use a 7mm barrel trimmer to square the ends of the blanks flush to the ends of the brass tubes.

5 Insert the mandrel into the headstock of the lathe and then place two 7mm spacer bushings onto the mandrel. Place the tip bushing first, then the lower barrel, then the center bushing, followed by the upper barrel, the cap bushing and the locking nut.

6 Reduce the pen blank to two cylinders using the roughing gouge. Shape the blanks using the skew or the spindlemaster, leaving the blanks slightly proud of the bushings.

7 Cut a ⁷⁄₃₂″ tenon into the lower portion of the upper barrel using a parting tool in the bevel cutting mode. This tenon is cut flush to the diameter of the center bushing to accommodate the center band.

8 Move the tool rest out of the way and use 220-grit sandpaper to sand the blanks flush with the bushings. Do not worry about the scratches; they will be removed in the next step using the padded aluminum oxide pads.

9 Start to smooth the pen with a green aluminum oxide pad. Follow with an orange pad, a purple pad, a blue pad and a gray pad.

10 Line up and assemble all the parts according to the instructions in the Comfort pen kit.

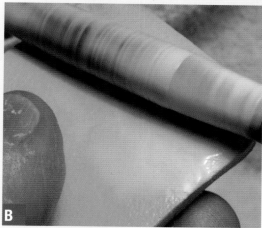

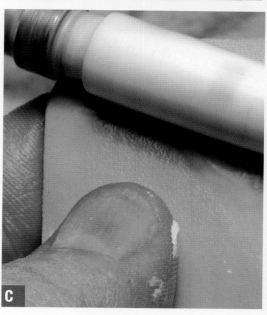

Project Four
Roller Ball Style Pen
Wood & Corian®

The classic style of a roller ball pen will be upgraded by using a Corian accent stripe placed in the upper tube. The upper and lower pen blanks of a classic style pen are turned straight across the grain and flush with the upper and lower bushings. These pieces can then be assembled with either a roller ball tip or a fountain pen nib depending upon which pen kit you choose. Both the fountain pen and the roller ball are turned the same way.

1 Add ¹⁄₁₆″ to each end and cut the pen blanks to the proper lengths, using the tubes as guides.

2 Cut the upper pen blank in half. Using a disc sander, place a 45-degree angle on the cuts.

3 Cut a small piece of Corian and sand one side to a matching 45-degree angle.

4 Use medium CA glue to attach a cut piece of Corian to one half of the pen blank. Sand the Corian flush with the side of the pen blank, then glue the other half of the blank together. Apply thin CA glue over the entire piece to fill any voids and add strength to the blank.

5 Drill the pen blanks with a 10mm brad point drill bit.

6 Continue to prepare the blanks as shown in Chapter 3. Square the ends of the pen blanks with a 10mm barrel trimmer.

7 Insert the mandrel into the headstock of the lathe and then place one 7mm spacer bushing onto the mandrel. Place the tip bushing, then the lower barrel, then the center bushing, followed by the upper barrel, the cap bushing and the locking nut.

8 Reduce your pen blank to two cylinders using the roughing gouge and then the skew or the spindlemaster. Turn the blanks completely straight across leaving them just proud of the bushings.

9 Measure ¹⁄₁₈″ from the bottom of the upper pen tube. Remove the material all the way down to the brass tube using a parting tool in the bevel cutting mode. Finish sanding the blanks using sandpaper up to 800-grit.

10 Start the finishing process with Triple EEE cream placed on a piece of cheese cloth. Follow this with the woodturner's finish applied with a paper towel. Remember to use the finishing material with a light touch on the bottom half of the pen blank.

11 Line up and assemble all the parts according to the instructions in the roller ball kit.

Project Five
Gelwriter Classic Click Style Pen
Deer Antler & Buffalo Horn

Turning a biological product such as buffalo horn or antler from deer, elk, antelope and moose is both rewarding and challenging to the turner. Each antler pen will be unique in its own right because no two antlers are alike.

Working with biological products offers the turner a unique set of challenges. One of the first challenges is the duality of the product. The interior of the antler is soft, and the outer surface is very hard. Drilling antler for pen tubes is easy; however, because the interior is so soft, a liberal amount of cyanoacrylate (CA) glue will be needed to ensure a good bond between the antler and the brass pen tube. Another challenge is finding a piece of antler that is straight enough to accommodate the length of the pen tube. Finally, any biological product when sanded, drilled or turned will emit an odor. Some people will find this odor displeasing. Use adequate ventilation in conjunction with a good dust collection system to assist with the evacuation of the odor.

Pen Tip

• Adequate ventilation and a dusk mask for odor control is a must.

• Use extra glue when gluing tubes into the antler blanks.

1 Add ¹⁄₁₆″ to each end and cut the pen blanks to the proper lengths, using the tubes as guides. Try to find two pieces of antler that are the same size.

2 To alleviate the problem of drilling the antler and other irregularly shaped objects off center, use a disc sander to sand one or more sides of the blank flat to assist the placement of the blanks into the drilling vise.

3 Use the pen vise with an 8mm high speed steel to drill a straight hole through the antler. Glue the tubes in, then square the ends of the pen blanks using an 8mm barrel trimmer.

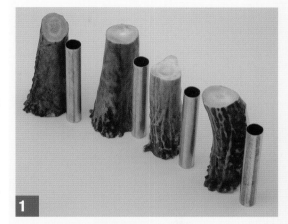

4 Insert the mandrel into the headstock of the lathe. Place one 7mm spacer bushing on the mandrel. Place one end bushing, then the lower barrel, then the center bushing, followed by the upper barrel, another end bushing and the locking nut.

5 Turn the hand wheel before the lathe is turned on to ensure that the tool rest does not strike the antler.

6 Reduce the speed of the lathe to around 600 rpm until the blanks are of uniform roundness. Then increase the lathe speed to 1800-2000 rpm. Only sharp tools will cut the hard exterior of the antler.

7 Slowly reduce the pen blank to two cylinders using the roughing gouge. Then, using the skew or the spindlemaster, turn the blanks straight across, leaving them just proud of the bushings. Use a straight edge to check the antler blank is straight across and does not have any bumps or humps.

8 Lightly sand the antler using 220, 320, 400 and 600-grit sandpaper. When the sanding is complete, blow the dust off the blanks with compressed air to remove any sanding particles that might fill the pores of the antler.

9 Apply Woodturner's Finish with a paper towel, lightly rubbing the towel back and forth until a small amount of heat is noticed on your finger. At that time you may start to apply more pressure to gain a deeper, richer shine.

Buffalo horn drills and cuts similar to antler.

10 Line up and assemble all the parts according to the instructions in the Slimline-Pro Gelwriter Click Style pen kit.

Project Six
Diagonal Dymondwood
Classic Elite Roller Ball

W hat is Dymondwood? Dymondwood is a technical marvel of wood and plastic composite. Hand-selected 1/16" hardwood veneers are impregnated with special dyes and plastic resins that are then laminated together under incredible heat and pressure to produce these special wooden blanks. The wood is then cut diagonally to form the unique patterns that are visible in the pen blanks.

Pen Tip

• Dymondwood is more dense than regular wood and some find it difficult to turn.

• Drill the blank carefully. Excessive heat from the drill will cause blow out.

• Use a light touch with your tools to avoid excessive tearout.

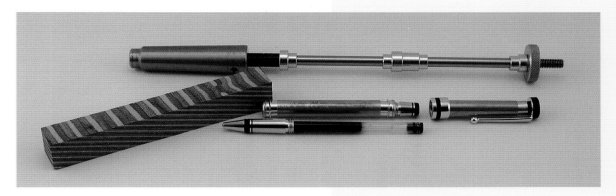

1 Add ¹⁄₁₆" to each end and cut the pen blanks to the proper lengths, using the tubes as guides.

2 Drill the blank with a 10mm high speed steel drill bit. A word of caution concerning Dymondwood: Avoid overheating the Dymondwood while drilling the blank. It will cause the pen blank to split apart (See Trouble shooting tips on page 66.)

3 Prepare the blank according to the directions in Chapter Three.

4 Square the ends of the Dymondwood pen blanks using a 10mm barrel trimmer.

5 Sharpen your tools before turning Dymondwood. Dymondwood uses a lot of glue to hold the ¹⁄₁₆" hardwood veneers together. These glues will rapidly dull your turning tools.

6 Insert the mandrel into the headstock of the lathe. Place one 7mm spacer bushing onto the mandrel. Place the tip bushing first, then the lower barrel, then the center bushing, followed by the upper barrel, the cap bushing and the locking nut.

7 Reduce the pen blank to two cylinders using the roughing gouge. Then, using the skew or the spindlemaster, turn the blanks completely straight across, leaving them just proud of the bushings. Use a straight edge to ensure that the Dymondwood blank is straight across and does not have any bumps or humps.

8 Use a ruler to mark a line ¹⁄₈" from the lower portion of the upper barrel. Remove the wood down to the brass tube using a parting tool in the bevel rubbing mode to accommodate the center band.

9 Lightly sand the Dymondwood using 220, 320, 400 & 600 grit sandpaper. When the sanding is completed, blow the dust off the blanks with compressed air to remove any sanding particles.

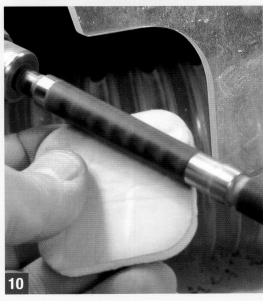

10 Finish sanding the blanks using sandpaper, up to 600 grit, or aluminum oxide pads without water. A light touch is needed when using these pads dry.

11 Apply Woodturner's Finish with a paper towel, lightly rubbing the towel back and forth until a small amount of heat is noticed on your finger. At that time you may start to apply more pressure to gain a deeper, richer appearing shine. Assemble per instructions for the Classic Elite Roller Ball.

Troubleshooting

In this chapter are some of the more common mistakes made by all pen turners. As you become more proficient in turning, these mistakes will become a distant memory of days past.

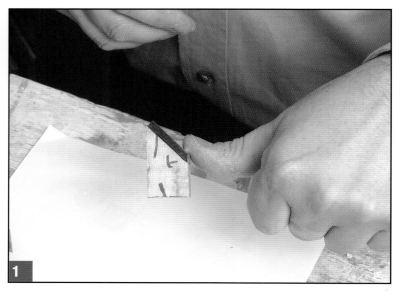

I glued my finger to the blank.

CA glue does not discriminate between wood and fingers. Use the utmost care when gluing as contact with your skin can cause serious injury. Follow the cautions from the manufacturer of the glue. (See Photo 1.)

My blank was damaged during drilling.

Make sure you are drilling down the center of the blank.

Avoid blowouts by removing chips often during drilling to cool heat build-up. (See Photo 2.)

My pen tube is not glued in correctly.

You'll need to start over. Use medium CA glue to gain a few extra seconds to coat the inside of the pen blank. (See Photo 3.)

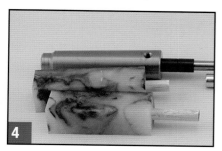

My brass pen tube shows through the finished pen.

On your next pen, paint the brass tube the same color as the pen blank, so the brass pen tube cannot show through the blank. (See Photo 4.)

My pen blank split while I was trimming it.

Slow down next time around. You were too aggressive using the barrel trimmer to square the blanks. (See Photo 5.)

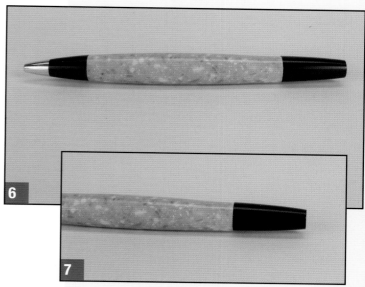

My finished pen is not round.

If the tail stock and/or the locking nut are too tight, it may cause the mandrel to be slightly out of round, which will not be apparent until the pen is assembled. (See Photos 6 and 7.)

Too much tool pressure may also be a culprit. Remember, a light touch is always better. You can always remove more material, but you can never put it back on!

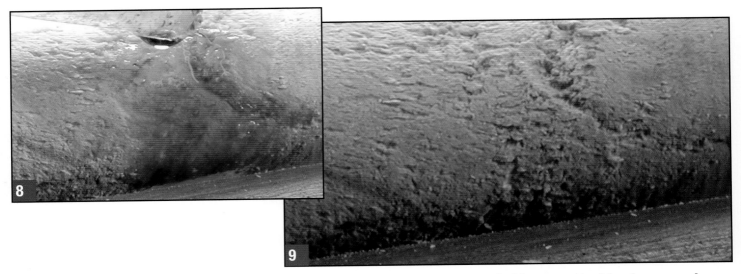

The "punky" material in my pen blank caused some tear-out.

When working with spalted wood or material that is very soft, place some thin CA glue right into the "punky" area of the wood. This will harden the material so it can be turned easily. (See Photos 8 and 9.)

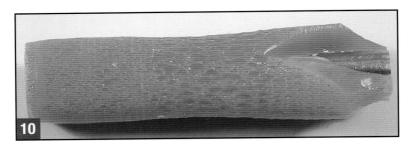

My acrylic pen blank is damaged beyond repair.

Go slow and easy on the next blank.
(See Photo 10.)

Should I disassemble my pen?

These are many reasons to disassemble a pen, here are just a few:

1. The refill is placed too deep in lower barrel. When assembling the twist mechanism into the pen blank be sure it is not inserted too deep.

2. The pen blank has separated from the pen tube. (See Photo 11.)

3. The end of the pen tube has cracked. (See Photo 12.)

How do I disassemble a pen?

1. Gather the tools to disassemble a pen. (See Photo 13.)

2. Place the thin rod through the twist mechanism and into the tip of the pen. Holding the barrel in one hand, gently tap the rod until the tip comes off. (See Photo 14.)

3. Place the thicker rod into the barrel and, on the other end, place the twist mechanism remover over the twist mechanism. Line the parts up as shown and press the twist mechanism out of the barrel. (See Photo 15.) You have successfully disassembled a pen.

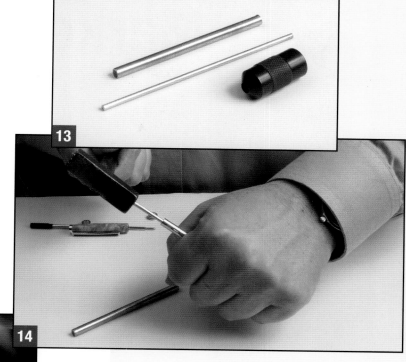

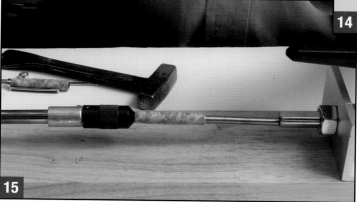

There is still glue left inside the pen tube even after I use the barrel trimmer.

Remove excess glue with an X-Acto® knife. (See Photo 16.)

Marketing Your Work

Cigar pens (left to right): lacewood, bocote, box elder and curly maple

So, you have made this one-of-a-kind, hand-crafted, stunning, spectacular, impressive pen. What do you do with it? Giving it to your mother, who appreciates anything you give her, may be gratifying at first; but, how many pens can she really use? Now that each member of your family and all your friends have at least six pens apiece, it may be time to think about selling your work. But how exactly do you do that?

There are books devoted to just this subject on how to market and sell your wooden creations. Therefore this section is by no means going to give you the silver bullet step-by-step key to success. However, it will offer some realistic ideas on how to sell your pens, how to present your work to your customers, how to price your work, and how to set realistic expectations from you and your turnings.

All kidding aside, this is probably the most important section of this book. Whether you are making pens with the specific objective of starting your own business or just selling them to earn extra money, the first rule is to be realistic. In all probability, you will not take an order for 1,000 pens your first week. The following few paragraphs should give you some general guidelines for marketing your work.

Wholesale versus Retail...

The first questions to arise concerns selling to individuals or distributors who then sell to single people. Ask yourself, do you want to sell your pens directly to the public or do you want to have a shop owner sell them for you? Selling retail to the public directly is hard work. You will need to obtain a tax number to collect sales tax, a store of some kind (actual or virtual), and many other items best addressed by a book on the business of selling.

Selling your pens wholesale to a gallery or craft shop will alleviate some of the problems associated with directly selling to the public. There are advantages to selling wholesale, but you have to find the right store that will sell you and your work.

Finding a market for your work

I am a sales manager with over 25 years experience training sales representatives how to "sell." The first objective that is stressed for any good sales representative is to listen. We have two ears and one mouth, so why do we talk twice as much as we listen? Listen to what your customer is telling you.

Take some time and conduct your own survey by visiting some local shops that sell pens. Ask questions and find out exactly what the public is buying. If you are thinking of making some Slimline pens and find out from the shop owner that not a single Slimline pen has been sold, then you have your answer as to what the public wants—or in this case, doesn't want. Do your homework.

Finding the correct location

How do you find the right store? Again, ask questions. How long have they been in business? What is their customer profile? Are their customers affluent? Is the store you are thinking about part of a large mall or is it a stand-alone shop? These are questions that you are entitled to ask. After all, you do want your work to be sold and, more importantly, to get paid for it, don't you?

When you are in the store, look around. See the quality of the other merchandise being offered and look at the prices. Is this in the range you want to sell your work? I personally place all my pens in "upscale" shops. Here, I know that the patrons can afford the price I want to charge for my pens.

Another thought is that I will not put my pens in a store that does not sell pens. I want competition. I want the customer to see the other craftsmanship and compare it to mine and see the quality they get when they purchase my pen!

Listen to your customer

Once you have a location in hand and your work is selling, go back and ask them, "What else is the public looking to purchase?" Your current customers are going to be your best customers because they know your work and understand the value of your craftsmanship. Do not keep selling them the same pens every month. Your sales may get stale and drop. Change is good. Change the material. Create a different style pen. There are seven different styles offered in this book, but there are many more from which you can choose. Give your wholesaler a guarantee on your craftsmanship, and I even exchange pens if they do not sell in a few months, keeping the stock fresh!

Getting established

A good way to establish yourself is to offer your work for local fundraising. The local ambulance squad was having a fundraiser, and I offered to split the proceeds of the sales of my pens as a donation to the ambulance squad. This accomplished three things. First, it was good to give to the ambulance squad by donating the profits to charity. Second, it established my work in the area and exposed me to many people that I would not have been exposed to before because the fundraiser was held in a large mall. And third, as a result, many other orders were taken for special pens to be delivered at a later time.

Local Festivals & Craft Shows...

There are many different types of craft shows. I choose the juried shows. People attending a

Classic Elite Roller Ball (left to right): bird's eye maple and bird's eye maple dyed with mahogany stain

juried show know that the work has been reviewed by other artisans and craftsmen and that it has attained a certain level of quality. You can charge more for your work at a juried show than at a local craft fair.

Before you can be a vender at a juried show, you will have to send slides of your work to be judged. Make sure that the slides you send are representative of your work and that the slides themselves are a good quality. If the slides you send are poor quality, your chances of getting into that show are also poor. Even though the pens you produce are very good, the judges are judging you by the slides you send, so make sure the quality of the slides do your pens justice.

Specializing in a particular material and market...

The pens that I create are mostly made from Corian and acrylics. By specializing in this material, I market my Corian pens to local fabricators who make the counter tops and install them in their customer's home. I tell the fabricator, "Wouldn't it be nice to give your customer a handmade pen to match his or her counter top?" I have more business than I can handle! This is matching the market to a particular need the customer did not even know he needed.

There are other examples, such as the boat builders using nothing but mahogany for the inside of their boats and, oh by the way, here is a pen to match the interior. Cigar stores selling humidors made of exotic woods is another example. Sell them a cigar-style pen to match whatever exotic wood the humidor is made from.

Be creative and use your own imagination to come up with other ideas to sell your works of art!

Customizing your pens...

I recently was commissioned to make a pen for

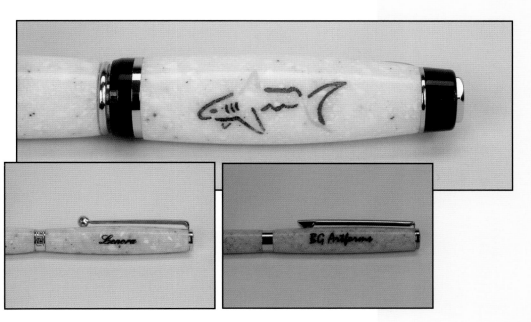

Greg Norman, the golfer. The customer wanted me to make a special pen just for him. I came up with the idea to place his trademarked logo on a pen for him. Engraving a pen with a logo is a simple way to customize the pen for an individual or a company. Pens can be engraved and then filled in with black or colored indelible markers.

Pricing your work...

I have saved the best for last. The first rule and best rule of selling, I truly believe, is placing a value on your time and sticking with it. How much should I charge for my pens? If I had a buck for every time I heard that, I would not have to write this book! The old adage—time is money—works here, too. Your time has a value. If someone picks up your pen and says that is too much money, do not argue. I tell them that they are right and that my pen is not for them. I am proud of my work and I am not ashamed to charge for it!

PRICE =
material cost + overhead + labor + profit

To the right are some issues to consider when trying to set a price for your pens. Some of you may not have all of the expenses that are listed there, but carefully take into consideration most of these items.

Material cost = cost of the pen kit + the cost of the pen blank. If you got the wood for nothing, then how about the gas it took to pick it up from your friend's house. Do not forget the time it took to retrieve these "free" pieces of wood.

Overhead = Heat, electric, rent, insurance, tools and other materials. If you are using your garage or another room in your house, you might want to factor in what that room actually costs you to maintain over the course of a year and then divide that by the number of pens you produce in a year.

Labor = How much is the local shop rate for a handy man in your area: $15.00, $20.00, $60.00 an hour? You will have to place a value on your time. Be realistic, but be fair to yourself!

Profit = Yes, profit, that dirty word that keeps our economy going! You are allowed to make money, and the person who is buying the pen from you knows you are making money. If the pen costs a certain amount after you figured out all of the other factors, a fair percentage to add to that number would be between 15%-20%. For example only, if you figure everything out and the cost is $24.00 then add between $3.60 and $4.80 for profit. So your cost to the customer would be about $29.00.

Corian Pens (left to right): two slimline pens, two Eurostyle pens, and one cigar pen.

Dymondwood Pens (left to right): roller ball, Eurostyle, cigar and comfort. Note that the pen blanks can be turned and centered so the Dymondwood pattern radiates outward.

Wood Pens (left to right): comfort, curly maple dyed blue; Eurostyle, curly maple dyed with a mahogany/red mix; roller ball, curly maple dyed red; roller ball, maple burl with mahogany stain.

InLace Pens: A mix of comfort and Eurostyle pens.

Click Pens (left to right): two pens turned from antler, one turned from buffalo horn.

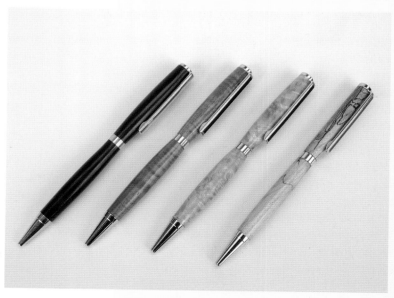

Slimlines Pens (left to right): ebony; curly maple dyed mahogany; maple burl; spalted maple.